MODELS OF HUMAN SEXUALITY AND SOCIAL CONTROL

Gene H. Starbuck

D1392072

UNIVERSITY
PRESS OF
AMERICA

Copyright © 1981 by

University Press of America, Inc.

P.O. Box 19101, Washington, D.C. 20036

Library of Congress Cataloging in Publication Data

Starbuck, Gene H.
    Models of human sexuality and social control.

    Bibliography: p.
    1. Sex (Psychology)   I. Title.
HQ21.S626   306.7   81-40136
ISBN 0-8191-1651-3   AACR2
ISBN 0-8191-1652-1 (pbk.)

DEDICATION

This book is dedicated to those who support the chasing of butterflies.

ACKNOWLEDGMENTS

This book has what seems to me to be a long history, especially considering its relative brevity. I began reading seriously in the field of human sexuality in 1975 as preparation to teach a course called "Sex Role Identification and Human Sexuality." The framework for the book began to take shape while I was doing pre-publication review and editing on the manuscript of John Gagnon's text, Human Sexualities. While there was no communication with him about the present work, his ideas have certainly influenced my own.

The first draft of the book was written while I was a participant in a 1978 National Endowment for the Humanities Summer Seminar, under the astute guidance of Mulford Q. Sibley, University of Minnesota. I wish to thank the NEH, Dr. Sibley, and the other seminar participants for that wonderful experience.

Blaine Mercer and Howard Higman, both at the University of Colorado, read an earlier draft of this work, and made helpful comments. Professor Higman has also been very influential to me in many other ways, both professionally and personally.

Finally, I would like to thank my mother, Ethel Starbuck, both for the many hours she spent typing and retyping the manuscript, and for the many years she and my father spent allowing me to make my own mistakes.

TABLE OF CONTENTS

INTRODUCTION

Every ongoing society must, in one way or another, take account of sexuality. Every society has a model of sexuality, just as there are models of religion and economics. The latter have received a good deal more attention from sociologists than has the former. This paper describes the major models of sexuality as found in Western societies.

The basic structure of the models is taken from Gagnon (1977), but has been altered and expanded. Each model has ways of answering certain basic questions about human sexuality: Is there in humans a strong sex drive? If so, what form does it take and should it be expressed or controlled? If not, how do humans become creatures who are sexual? What purposes does sexuality serve? What controls, if any, should be placed on sexual expression, and why? What view of human nature is implied by the model?

Three general models are proposed, each having specific sub-types. There are three control-repression models: traditional, Freudian, and sociological. The two expression models are nature-limited and natural diverse. Two learning models are discussed, mechanistic and social. The paper concludes by using the social learning model to analyze the social control implications of the other models.

CONTROL REPRESSION MODELS

The three control-repression models have similar implications for social control, although they arrive at their conclusions via different theoretical paths. All three assume the existence of a powerful, innate sex drive, and all three postulate that this drive must be tightly controlled. Each has generally assumed, whether implicitly or explicitly, that males somehow have a more powerful sex drive than females, and all three assume male dominance.

Traditional Control-Repression Model

This model is based primarily on a particular interpretation of the Bible and is supported by the writings of certain Christian theologians. The Old Testament indicates that the Israelites were influenced by several other groups with which they came in contact. They sometimes accepted and other times strongly rejected the customs to which they were exposed. Since the Old Testament is written at various times in Judaic history, under different social conditions, it is not entirely consistent. The same is true, of course, for the New Testament. St. Paul, for example, was under the impression that the end of the world was at hand. This leads him to give very different advice from that which he might have given had he been preparing people for a long struggle against the evils of this world.

Not all people, however, have the same view of the Bible. It is a matter of debate what St. Paul really intended to say; in what context he wrote; whether his writings are the word of God; why he wrote them; and why they were canonized. While these are certainly interesting questions, they do not primarily concern us here. What is important is that they are believed by many to be the word of God. Since it is what people believe to be true that influences their behavior, Paul's writings are important here because many people believe them and act accordingly.

People who accept the traditional control-repression model, then, believe that this passage by Paul (I Corinthians 7:1-9) should govern their behavior:

> Now concerning the matters about which you wrote. It is well for a man not to touch a woman. But because of the temptation to immorality, each man should have his own wife, and each woman her own husband. The husband should give to his wife her conjugal rights, and likewise the wife to her husband. For the wife does not rule over her own body, but the husband does; likewise the husband does not rule over his own body, but the wife does. Do not refuse one another except perhaps by agreement for a season, that you may devote yourself to prayer; but then come together again, lest Satan tempt you through lack of self-control. I say this by way of concession, not of command. I wish that all were as I myself am [celebate]. But each has his own special gift from God, one of one kind and one of another.
>
> To the unmarried and the widows I say that it is well for them to remain single as I do. But if they cannot exercise self-control, they should marry. For it is better to marry than to be aflame with passion. (Emphasis added.)

The implications are clear: there is a sex drive, which is a tool of Satan; some people are not as strong as Paul, and will submit; and the only proper context for this submission is in marriage. There is a hierarchy of sexual acceptability: highest of these is celibacy; second is

4

monogamous heterosexual activity (later defined as missionary-position sex for reproductive purposes only); lowest is all other sexual activity, which is sinful.

Traditional control-repressionists are fond also of using Paul as their spokesman on subordination of women. A common source is Ephesians 5:22-24:

> Wives, be subject to your husbands, as to the Lord. For the husband is the head of the wife as Christ is the head of the Church, his body, and is himself its Savior. As the Church is subject to Christ, so let wives also be subject in everything to their husbands.

The notion of male dominance is, of course, not peculiar to the early Christians. It existed in most early historical cultures, including the Babylonian, Egyptian, Judaic, Greek, Roman and others which influenced Christianity.

The importance of the patriarchal family unit is affirmed also in statements regarding adultery, including the Seventh Commandment (Exodus 20:14): "You shall not commit adultery." The New Testament further tightens the regulation. Jesus is quoted in Matthew 5:27-28:

> You have heard that it was said, "You shall not commit adultery." But I say to you that everyone who looks at a woman lustfully has already committed adultery with her in his heart. If your right eye causes you to sin, pluck it out and throw it away; it is better that you lose one of your members than that your whole body be thrown into hell.

It is not now sufficient to act properly; one must also think clean thoughts. Since there are few who are not guilty of an occasional evil thought, guilt is guaranteed. This point will arise again when we discuss Freud.

Concern for the traditional family also governed Biblical injunctions regarding premarital sex. To the Hebrews, the value of a daughter was that she could fetch a bride-price when married or even, in cases of extreme debt, be sold into an attenuated form of slavery (Exodus 21). As with other goods, the bride would not bring top price if she were damaged property. The groom, upon finding that his bride was not a virgin, could have her stoned to death by the men of the city. However, if her father could produce the "tokens of her virginity" (presumably a blood-stained sheet or undergarment), he could have the false accuser whipped and fined for besmirching <u>his</u> reputation.

For the unmarried male, the rules were somewhat different. Although it was considered unwise, consorting with fallen women or prostitutes from other tribes was not forbidden. After all, that was better than rape or adultery. But care must still be taken; in Proverbs 6:26 the man is advised "Do not desire her beauty in your heart, and do not let her capture you with her eyelashes; for a harlot may be hired for a loaf of bread, but an adulteress stalks a man's very life."

In the New Testament, Paul would have none of this. He countenanced neither premarital sex (better to marry than to burn) nor prostitution. In a sense, Paul provided for woman more security, if not equality, than was found in the Hebraic customs. Divorce was not acceptable, so the woman had security in the home.

In light of the contemporary debate about homosexuality, it is important to discover the traditional control-repression doctrine on this topic. The story of Lot in the cities of Sodom and Gomorrah (Genesis 19 and 20) is often given as justification of opposition to homosexuality. It seems Lot took some angels in as overnight

6

visitors. The angels must have been terribly
attractive, for soon the men of Sodom were banging
on Lot's door, demanding that he send out the
visitors so they might "know" them. Lot offered
to give the unruly mob his two virgin daughters
instead, but they refused the compromise. Finally
the angels blinded them, and they went away.
Their crime was so heinous that the entire city
had to be destroyed. Sodomy, then, became the
term not only for homosexuality but has been
extended to include oral and anal sex and
bestiality.

It is interesting that a story very similar
to that of Lot is told in Judges 19. This time
the guest is not an Angel, but a mere mortal.
When the mob pounds on the door, the host offers
both his virgin daughter and his concubine. At
first the mob rejects the offer, but when the host
shoves the concubine out the door to them, they
make do with her: "and they knew her, and abused
her all night until morning. And as the dawn
began to break, they let her go. And as morning
appeared, the woman came and fell down at the door
of the man's house where her master was, till it
was light." Although these men were punished,
they escaped the destruction to which Sodom was
subjected. Perhaps because they were bisexual
rather than homosexual their punishment was
lighter.

Much of the Judaic response to homosexuality
was a reaction to surrounding cults which prac-
ticed homosexual prostitution (Deuteronomy 23:
17-18): "There shall be no cult prostitute . . .
of the sons of Israel. You shall not bring the
hire of a harlot, or the wages of a dog [homo-
sexual prostitute], into the house of Yahweh your
God, in payment for any vow, for both of these are
an abomination to Yahweh your God." The references
in Leviticus (18:22) are more specific to homosexuality itself: "You shall not lie with a male
as with a woman: it is an abomination." Even
more harsh is Leviticus 20:13: "If a man lies
with a male as with a woman, both of them have

committed an abomination; they shall be put to death, their blood is upon them."

Some of the opposition to homosexuality must have come from support for the patriarchal family and the strong distinction between masculinity and femininity (Cole, 1959). Deuteronomy 22:5 supports this view: "A woman shall not wear anything that pertains to a man, nor shall a man put on a woman's garment; for whoever does these things is an abomination to Yahweh your God." It might be noted in passing that those who support the traditional control-repression model are somewhat selective as to their use of Biblical authority. In Deuteronomy 21, just a few verses prior to the above quote, is the rule that children who are rowdy and disobey their parents should be taken outside the city and stoned to death. Anita Bryant has been curiously quiet on this law.

The traditional control-repression model opposes both masturbation and birth control. Since there is very little in the Bible to support these positions, the story of Onan has had to do double duty. According to the custom of the Levirate, if a man died without male issue, his brother was to conceive with the widow so that the dead man's lineage would not die out. Onan's brother died, and Genesis 38:8-10 tells the rest of the story:

> Then Judah said to Onan, "Go in to your brother's wife, and perform the duty of a brother-in-law to her, and raise up offspring for your brother." But Onan knew that the offspring would not be his; so when he went in to his brother's wife he spilled the semen on the ground, lest he should give offspring to his brother. And what he did was displeasing in the sight of the Lord, and he slew him also.

Though many Biblical scholars (cf. Kosnik et al, 1977) argue that Onan's sin was actually breaking the Levirate custom, the verse has been used to

8

support opposition to both birth control (coitus interruptus) and masturbation (Onanism).

Many other verses in the Bible discuss sex-related topics. There are frequent references to adultery, prostitution, incest, and bestiality; the first two are not always condemned. Most of the verses commonly referred to by the traditional control-repressionists have been mentioned. A word of caution is in order, however. There is no reason to believe that all early Christians interpreted them in this way, or even knew about them. Later writers, such as St. Augustine (354-430) and St. Thomas Aquinas (1225-1274) added weight to them; but they may not have affected the majority of Christians in the discussed form until several centuries later.

The life of St. Augustine parallels, in many ways, that of Paul. Both were, by their own retrospective admissions, evil young men. Both had striking conversions and became important control-repressionists. It was after reading Paul that Augustine, then thirty-two, was finally convinced to become celibate. His The City of God was an important influence on the Roman Catholic Church. Katchedourian (1971:534) summarizes Augustine's views on sexuality:

> He acknowledges that coitus is essential to the propagation of mankind, but argues that the act itself is tainted with guilt because of the sin of Adam and Eve. . . . Whereas St. Paul had viewed the married state as inferior to celibacy on the grounds that it was distracting for those who truly wanted to dedicate themselves to God, St. Augustine went a step further and labeled intercourse, even within marriage, as sinful. . . . Although one could minimize the sinfulness of coitus by performing it only as part of fulfilling one's duty to have children . . . one could not totally ignore the fact that a child conceived under these

9

circumstances is the product of an act of concupiscence. Hence the need for infant baptism in order to wash away the guilt of lust as well as of Original Sin.

It has often been pointed out that Christ's life confirms these views. He was born without original sin (virgin birth) and lived a pure life (celibate). He did not, presumably, even masturbate; nor did he talk much about sex.

St. Thomas Aquinas provides much more specific arguments for the traditional control-repression model. He drew not only from the Bible and church fathers for his sources, but also relied on "natural law" and the use of "right reason." His work was quite thorough, as Katchedourian (1971:536) indicates:

> There is virtually no form of sexual behavior to which Aquinas did not address himself. In his massive work Summa Theologica he has included dissertations on touching, kissing, fondling, seduction, intercourse, adultery, fornication, marriage, virginity, homosexuality, incest, rape, bestiality, prostitution, and related topics.

In one rather complicated discourse he determined that "noctural pollution" is not itself sinful, but is often caused by a previous sin on the part of the polluter; therefore it is an indication of sin. Simple fornication (premarital sex) is a mortal sin because it may deprive a potential child of the advantages of growing up with both a mother and a father.

Aquinas's use of natural law to support his points was not new; it was a method used by Aristotle. The method was used by both men to the same end in regard to the status of women. It is obvious, argued both men, that males are stronger and more intelligent than women, but that women are well equipped for conceiving and raising

10

children. Natural law dictates, then, that women be subordinate to men and concern themselves with matters of home and children while men attend to the tasks of politics, property, and other important issues. When later the church gradually gave way to science, the natural law argument became a very popular one to support a wide variety of causes.

Lest we leave the impression that traditional control-repressionism has only old texts for support, more recent documents will be mentioned. For those who would overcome, by using birth control, Aquinas's well-reasoned argument against premarital sex, Pope Paul VI (1968) has an answer:

> Not much experience is needed in order to know human weakness, and to understand that men--especially the young, who are so vulnerable on this point--have need of encouragement to be faithful to the moral law, so that they must not be offered some easy means of eluding its observance. It is also to be feared that the man, growing used to the employment of anticonception practices, may finally lose respect for the woman and, no longer caring for her physical and psychological equilibrium, may come to the point of considering her as a mere instrument of selfish enjoyment, and no longer as his respected and beloved companion.

This passage also points out that men seem to have a stronger sex drive. There is no worry that women will consider men "merely as instruments of selfish enjoyment." The sex drive appears also to be strongest in the young "who are so vulnerable on this point."

In case this vulnerable young man should be tempted to resort to masturbation, the 1976 Catholic Declaration on Certain Questions Concerning Sexual Ethics (in Kosnik et al, 1977) has a

11

prohibition against that too:

> Whatever the force of certain arguments of a biological and philosophical nature, which have sometimes been used by theologians, in fact both the magisterium of the Church--in the course of a constant tradition--and the moral sense of the faithful have declared without hesitation that masturbation is an intrinsically and seriously disordered act.
>
> The main reason is that, whatever the motive for acting in this way, the deliberate use of the sexual faculty outside the normal conjugal relations essentially contradicts the finality of the faculty. For it lacks the sexual relationship called for by the moral order, namely the relationship which realizes the "full sense of mutual self-giving and human procreation in the context of true love."
>
> All deliberate exercise of sexuality must be reserved to this regular relationship. Even if it cannot be proved that Scripture condemns this sin by name, the tradition of the Church has rightly understood it to be condemned in the New Testament when the latter speaks of "impurity," "unchasteness" and other vices contrary to chastity and continence. . . . The frequency of the phenomenon in question is certainly to be linked with man's innate weakness following original sin; but it is also to be linked with the loss of a sense of God, with the corruption of morals engendered by the commercialization of vice, with the unrestrained licentiousness of so many public entertainments and publications as well as with the neglect of modesty, which is the guardian of chastity.

This last quote indicates another characteristic of the control-repression model: it is better not to expose people to things which might tempt them. This seems to imply that the more the sex drive is exposed or expressed, the stronger it becomes; which has led to opposition to sex education, "pornography," certain styles of dress and music, and other potential corrupters.

Although the Catholic Church has been perhaps the most consistent supporter of the traditional control-repression model, it is by no means the only one. Protestantism, from Calvin through contemporary fundamentalism, has certainly contributed to the support of this model, although sometimes disagreeing on the issue of birth control. Originally through the influence of the churches, and later through "science," this model has been the foundation for most of the laws governing sexual morality of the Western world, perhaps especially in the United States. It became the dominant model of Victorianism in the nineteenth century, and influenced much secular and scientific thought about sexuality. Many of the sexologists, then, provide the historical bridge to the Freudian control-repression model.

The Freudian Control-Repression Model

Our "great person" view of history often leads us to believe that important ideas arise, sui generis, from great thinkers. But all great thinkers build on that which has gone before, and Sigmund Freud is no exception. Freud's concept of the libido, for example, can be compared to the Christian "original sin," and Christian dualism has its parallel in Freud's conflict between the individual's instincts and society, and between the id and superego. There were also Freudian precursors in the sciences.

The Swiss physician, S. A. Tissot, was one who anticipated a crucial element in Freud's theories (Gagnon, 1977). Tissot's 1758 Onania, or a Treatise Upon the Disorders Produced by Masturbation professed the view that semen was a fluid, limited in quantity, and necessary for bodily health. If a man were to expend it recklessly, he would become weak and listless, and would not have the energy necessary to do useful work. The list of purported ills of masturbation, both before and after Tissot wrote, is a long one (Katchadourian, 1972:282):

> Insanity; epilepsy; various forms of headaches (in addition to "strange sensations at the top of the head"); numerous eye diseases (including dilated pupils, dark rings around the eyes, "eyes directed upward and sideways"); intermittent deafness; redness of nose and nosebleeds; hallucination of smell and hearing; "morbid changes in the nose"; hypertrophy and tenderness of the breasts; afflictions of the ovaries, uterus, and vagina (including painful menstruation and "acidity of the vagina"); pains of various kinds, specifically "tenderness of the skin in the lower dorsal region;" asthma; heart murmurs ("masturbator's heart"); and skin ailments ranging from acne to wounds, pale and discolored skin, and "an undesirable odor of the skin in women" are all supposed consequences of masturbation."[1]

---

[1] It is not difficult to see how these misjudgments could have been made. Almost everyone had masturbated, but almost no one readily admitted it. A physician or psychologist, suspecting that masturbation was the cause of a particular malady, would ask its sufferer if he or she ever masturbated. Sure enough, most of them did, so his theory was confirmed. Of course those who said they did not masturbate were assumed to be lying, so the theory stood. What the enquirer failed to do was ask healthy people if they masturbated. This methodological problem still plagues the clinical approach to sexual studies.

Tissot's views had implications beyond masturbation. <u>Any</u> sexual activity (at least any which led to orgasm) would deplete the vital juices. In this regard, then, sexual intercourse in marriage was no different from masturbation, adultery, or premarital sex. This theory was later popularized in the United States by William Alcott,[2] a co-healthian of Sylvester Graham (Graham bread). Alcott (in Ditzion, 1969:324), writing in the 1830's, believed that

> Even marriage before the age of physical maturity--twenty-five or twenty-six for the male; twenty-one or twenty-two for the female--involved the danger of depleting one's supply of vital juices. For every year of precocious indulgence, one would decline three years earlier.

This view has survived into the twentieth century. A 1913 book called <u>Sexual Knowledge</u> (in Gagnon, 1977:148) is quite similar:

> We must also note the fact that every procreative act is performed at a sacrifice of some of the vital fluid on the part of the male. A wanton sacrifice of some of the vital fluid, either in the act of self-abuse or excessive indulgence in the sexual act, is not justifiable under any consideration. In the light of these facts, every normal man will admit that frequent masturbation or excessive sexual intercourse, in wedlock or out, would certainly not be recommended as a method of developing the sex apparatus.

Indeed, the current myths that an athlete should

---

[2]William was the brother of Amos Bronson Alcott, a founder of Fruitlands commune and father of Louisa May Alcott, who wrote <u>Little Women</u>.

refrain from sex the night before the big game, and that a man is "naturally" sleepy after sex, can be seen as a folk manifestation of the same view.

This notion of vital juices has definite implications regarding the status of women in society. If sperm is a vital juice the loss of which prevents a man from fully realizing his productive capacity, and women have no sperm to begin with, it would follow that women innately lack the productive capacity of men. As will be seen, the vital juices theory is, in somewhat disguised form, an important component of Freud's theories.

Economic thought has also found its way into beliefs about sexuality. The eighteenth century was important for the growth of capitalism as an economic model. Adam Smith's Wealth of Nations was published in 1776 and buttressed folk justifications of capitalism, such as Ben Franklin's "a penny saved is a penny earned." Since sexuality tends to be talked about in the language which surrounds it, it is not surprising that the capitalist metaphor was applied, in the context of Puritanism, to sex. Gagnon (1975:16) writes, "When capitalism came along, sex got bound up in the economic ethic--prudence instead of profligacy, privatization instead of public display, savings instead of expenditures." In Victorian erotic writing, the common verb meaning orgasm was "to spend." This notion is not only related to capitalism, but is closely associated with the vital juices theories. To be a wise investor, then, one does not spend one's capital in a foolish manner, but only where it will draw the most interest. A man may or may not, then, choose to invest in his wife.

Other fields of study also contributed to what was to become the Freudian control-repression model. Malthus had, in 1796, published his Essay on the Principles of Population, with his famous warning that the fast growing population would soon outstrip the food available to feed itself.

As a capitalist, he supported private property; as a clergyman he prescribed late marriages and moral restraint instead of birth control; as a pessimist he did not have a good deal of faith in either of these methods, and left it largely to war, famine and disease to solve the problem that the reproductive drive was causing.

Herbert Spencer (in Ditzion, 1969), who drew sociology and Darwin together into social Darwinism, was more optimistic on this point. Brain work, he felt, drew much of the energy from the sex drive (vital juices). Since societies were becoming increasingly more complex, and complex societies require more brain work, population would become self-limiting as brain work replaced the reproductive drive.

It was in the framework of these and other ideas that Freud, writing in Victorian Vienna, Austria, formulated his well-known views on sexuality. Although the consequences for social control of his and the traditional control-repression model were similar, it would be a mistake to assume that this similarity was stressed by proponents of either view. Indeed, they often considered themselves to be at polar opposites. One of Freud's first important works, Three Essays on the Theory of Sexuality, postulated the existence of infant sexuality. The reaction to these views, among both the general public and his medical peers, was one of shocked disbelief. The similarity of this to the doctrine of Original Sin was not noticed by either party. Freud had other arguments with religion in general and Christianity in particular. He sometimes referred to religion as "infantilism" and considered the commandment to "Love thy neighbor as thyself" as both impossible and destructive to the individual psyche.

Interpreting Freud is much like interpreting the Bible. One can misquote, misinterpret, and select passages to prove a widely divergent set of views. Freud's theories were constantly evolving;

17

many theories were tentatively put forth, and then withdrawn as his "evidence" seemed to prove them wrong. His views of the human instincts were particularly vulnerable on this point. He wrote, at various times, about a hunger instinct; an aggression instinct; a death instinct; and an Eros instinct. There can be little doubt, though, that the sex instinct was by far the most important.

The name given to the energy produced by the instincts in the individual was the libido, which was located in a part of the ego called the id. The infant was born with the id, and little else. Gradually the infant learned to distinguish itself from the outside, or not-self. Thus were the boundaries of the ego drawn around the id. The function of the ego, which operated on the reality principle, was to negotiate between the self and not-self to achieve the gratification of the libido. The Father (the representative of external repression of the libido) would not allow total gratification of the instincts. At first the organism was only concerned about getting caught in its forbidden gratification. Gradually, however, the external prohibitions become internalized in the form of the superego. The individual must then be concerned not only about getting caught, but about doing the forbidden act at all; indeed, the mere intention of doing the forbidden was enough to produce the guilt by which the superego reigned. (Notice the similarity between this last notion and the Biblical "I say to you that everyone who looks at a woman lustfully has already committed adultery with her in his heart.")

One of the first confrontations between libidinal drives and external authority to be negotiated by the individual is the Oedipal Complex, in which the male child desires to have sex with his mother and kill his rival, the father. (The analogous problem for the female infant, about which Freud wrote very little, is sometimes called the Electra Complex.) The power of the father has created the incest taboo, so the satisfaction of the libido in its first object is thwarted. The

18

libido, throughout the individual's life, is constantly met with frustration in its attempts at gratification.

In his later works (Totem and Taboo, 1913; The Future of an Illusion, 1927; and Civilization and its Discontents, 1930), Freud extends his analysis of culture. His essential premise is that the desires of the individual and the demands of civilization are, by their very natures, in constant conflict. The libido wants constant gratification of its wishes, which would be to "rape, pillage, and plunder." Thus would individuals always be in conflict with each other, and rule by the strongest would prevail. So the individual libido gives up some of its gratification for the more secure position provided by civilization. The individual is hence protected, but also repressed. This view is similar to that proposed by Hobbes in the Leviathon. To Hobbes, life in its natural state is "nasty, brutish, and short." So humans enter into an inviolable contract with the state as a means of protection.

The subordination of libido to civilization occurs gradually and in many different specifics. The taming of fire was certainly a large step in the direction of civilization, but was not without its consequences. In a footnote in Civilization and its Discontents (p.37) Freud hypothesizes:

> It is as though primal man had the habit, when he came in contact with fire, of satisfying an infantile desire connected with it, by putting it out with a stream of his urine. The legends that we possess leave no doubt about the originally phallic view taken of tongues of flame as they shoot upwards. Putting out fire by micturating--a theme to which modern giants, Gulliver in Lilliput and Rabelais' Gargantua, still hark back-- was therefore a kind of sexual act with a male, an enjoyment of sexual potency in a homosexual competition. The first person

to renounce this desire and spare the fire
was able to carry it off with him and sub-
due it to his own use. By damping down
the fire of his own sexual excitation, he
had tamed the natural force of fire. This
great cultural conquest was thus the reward
for his renunciation of instinct. Further,
it is as though woman had been appointed
guardian of the fire which was held cap-
tive on the domestic hearth, because her
anatomy made it impossible for her to
yield to the temptation of this desire.

The most important conflict on the path to
civilization, however, was the killing of the
father. In the original primal horde, it was the
father who, being the strongest, ruled. The
brothers eventually discovered that if they would
cooperate they were stronger in a group than the
father was by himself. In thus banding together
they either killed the father or got rid of him in
some other way. If they killed him, they felt
guilty; if they did not kill him but only thought
about it, they still felt guilty. In either case
they had taken one giant step toward both civilization and perpetual guilt. This view parallels, in
the historical sense, the Christian "original sin."

Other factors were at work to create the
family. When the sexual urge of the male became
constant, rather than seasonal, Freud (1930:78)
believed

the male acquired a motive for keeping
the female, or, speaking more generally,
his sexual objects, near him; while the
female, who did not want to be separated
from her helpless young, was obliged, in
their interests, to remain with the
stronger male.

In the family, the power of specific genital sexuality broadened into the more general power of
love. It became fixated on specific love objects,
which renders the libido subject not only to

repression but vulnerable to the loss of the love object. Further complications, says Freud (1930: 50), arose:

> Women soon come into opposition to civilization and display their retarding and restraining influence--those very women who, in the beginning, laid the foundations of civilization by the claims of their love. Women represent the interests of the family and of sexual life. The work of civilization had become increasingly the business of men, it confronts them with ever more difficult tasks and compels them to carry out instinctual sublimations of which women are little capable. Since a man does not have unlimited quantities of psychical energy at his disposal, he has to accomplish his tasks by making an expedient distribution of his libido. What he employs for cultural aims he to a great extent withdraws from women and sexual life. His constant association with men, and his dependence on his relations with them, even estrange him from his duties as a husband and father. Thus the woman finds herself forced into the background by the claims of civilization and she adopts a hostile attitude towards it.

In a nutshell, this quote provides Freud's relevant views on civilization. Man has only limited libidinal energy (vital juices). The demands of civilization draw some of the energy from pure gratification. The poor woman can only sit on the sidelines. ("Wives be subject to your husbands.") It remains to be determined, however, exactly how it is that civilization draws its libidinal energy. To do this also requires a description of the characteristics of civilization.

One characteristic of civilization is love of beauty. Freud admits that he is not sure how this love originates. This lack of knowledge, however,

will never keep a man like Freud (1930:30) from
guessing:

> All that seems certain is its derivation
> from the field of sexual feeling. The
> love of beauty seems a perfect example
> of an impulse inhibited in its aim.
> "Beauty" and "attraction" are originally
> attributes of the sexual object. It is
> worth remarking that the genitals them-
> selves, the sight of which is always
> exciting, are nevertheless hardly ever
> judged to be beautiful; the quality of
> beauty seems, instead, to attach to cer-
> tain secondary sexual characters.

Another important characteristic of civilization is cleanliness and order. The origin of this
in the individual is more clear. Young human beings have an innate anal erotism, but this interest is soon repressed (Freud, 1930:43):

> Their original interest in the excretory
> function, its organs and products, is
> changed in the course of their growth
> into a group of traits which are familiar
> to us as parsimony, a sense of order and
> cleanliness--qualities which, though
> valuable and welcome in themselves, may
> be intensified till they become markedly
> dominant and produce what is called the
> anal character.

Certain kinds of activities and products,
then, are socially desirable. The libido, in
civilization, is not allowed, either by external
forces or by the superego, its immediate gratification. This unspent energy builds up in the
individual. Through the process of sublimation,
the energy is redirected from its natural gratification and into the socially acceptable forms.
In this way arise the important institutions of
religion, politics, and art. But sublimation,
while releasing energy, is never as satisfying as
more direct gratification in its natural form.

Furthermore, not all individuals are capable of productive sublimation. This produces a malaise, or discontent; the individual who would not survive without civilization, can never be completely happy with it.

The implications of Freud's theories for social control of sexuality become obvious. The individual has a certain amount of libidinal energy about which something must be done. To allow free expression of these drives would render civilization impossible. Pornography and masturbation would allow for release of the drives, but would deprive the civilizing forces of much of their energy; so these potential outlets must be controlled or eliminated. Homosexuality is either a perversion or an illness, a result of improper negotiation of the Oedipal problem. It might be amenable to psychotherapy, but should certainly be discouraged. Adultery threatens the generalized love which holds the family together, so it too should be avoided. Women have less libidinal energy, and that which they do have is used up in the family. They have none left for sublimation for wider cultural achievement; their place is in the home. In short, the social control implications of the Freudian control-repression model are nearly identical to those of the traditional control-repression model, but they are arrived at via different theoretical routes. The same is largely true of the sociological control-repression model.

Sociological Control-Repression Model

Support for the sociological control-repression model comes from two branches of sociological thought: sociobiology and functionalism. The former blends into and supports the latter. Sociobiology has much in common with the precursors of the Freudian model as it was discussed above. Kenneth Boulding (1978:260) summarizes this view as follows: "In its origin, sociobiology was an attempt . . . to expand the

23

Darwinian (or, perhaps one should say the neo-
Darwinian) model of evolutionary dynamics to explain animal behavior as well as animal morphology."
Edward O. Wilson (1975, 1978), considered to be
the modern founder of sociobiology, dealt primarily
with "societies" which exist in nonhuman species;
but it is with his attempt to extend his analysis
to humans (Wilson is a zoologist) that concerns us
most here.

Wilson's approach contains three basic elements, none of which are either new or unique to
sociobiology: attribution of animal characteristics to humans; biological or genetic determinism;
and anthropomorphism.

The attempt to understand humans by applying
to them knowledge gained by studying animals is at
least as old as Aristotle and St. Thomas Aquinas,
who sought in the animal world a "natural law"
which could then be applied to the human world.
More contemporary uses of this method are cloaked
in the mantle of science, rather than natural law.
From biology, for example, Ardrey has argued that
territoriality (1966) and dominance (1970) are
universal animal characteristics; and since humans
are animals, these characteristics explain human
behavior as well. Psychology has contributed
Skinner (1938) and others who apply animal learning processes to humans. One branch of anthropology, too, uses this method. LaBarre (1954), for
example, begins his study of humans with a discussion of one-celled animals, then moves through
various evolutionary stages of development to
humans. In doing so, he provides an excellent
example of a sociobiologic approach by extending
causes of animal behavior to humans.

Biological or genetic determinism, the second
characteristic of sociobiology, is also a common
approach in other fields. Freud, as previously
discussed, argued that "biology is destiny," particularly as applied to sex roles. Jensen (1969)
and others have argued that intelligence is
genetically determined and varies by race,

24

accounting for at least part of the difference in achievement between blacks and whites in the United States. Lorenz (1966) has argued that aggression is an innate animal and human characteristic, accounting not only for war and other violence, but for differences between men and women as well.

Anthropomorphism is the third characteristic of sociobiology. In the process of extending knowledge of animal behavior to humans, human characteristics are often extended to animals as well. This results in a blurring of the distinction between humans and other species. For example, in a discussion of the difference between asexual and sexual reproduction, Barash (1977:139) observes that asexual reproduction produces genetically identical offspring; but

> In contrast, sexual reproduction produces genetically distinct offspring, thus introducing self versus other into the biological world. By generating individuality and hence opening the door to selfish competition between individuals whose personal strategies often conflict, sexuality would seem to constitute further hazard to those would-be parents who adopt this particular strategy of reproduction.

Several points are implied by this quote. First, it seems to imply that animals as low in the phylogenetic scale as, say, fruit flies, can comprehend the notion of "individuality" and act upon it; that they can develop a "strategy" based on a notion of selfish competition; that they have "parents;" and finally, in some teleological fashion, a particular species has "adopted" (i.e., chosen) a particular form of reproduction. Sociobiologists would deny that these implications are at all intended; but their works are permeated with language that leaves the impression that they find it perfectly appropriate to extend human characteristics either to the evolutionary process itself, to species as a whole, or to specific

25

animals within a species.

Given these three characteristics of sociobiologic thought, then, it is not surprising the
conclusions that are drawn regarding human sexuality and the roles of men and women. Although
LaBarre's The Human Animal was written in 1954,
prior to the wide use of the term sociobiology,
that book seems to capture the essence of the
sociobiologic argument as it applies to the subject at hand. LaBarre's general argument runs as
follows: the thing that makes humans most human
is their use of language and symbols; this is made
possible by culture; but culture is only made possible by the family; and the family is possible
only because of certain innate characteristics of
human males, females, and infants. The foundation
of all that is human, then, rests on the sex drive
in the male, the maternal instinct of the female,
and the prolonged helplessness of the infant.

Humans (male humans, at least) do have a sex
drive; but the nature of that drive is somewhat
unclear. For example, LaBarre (1954:210) argues:
". . . it is a genital and not a philoprogenitive
drive that does it. The human male has no instincts, no anatomy, and no physiology to teach
him to love the child as such." However, just six
lines earlier, he states, "Man uses the family in
the service of his heightened instinctual needs."
At any rate, man has a sex drive which is different from other animals in that it is not seasonal
but constant. This leads him to acquire a relatively permanent mate (or mates), since that is
easier than to be constantly seeking out sexual
partners.

The male, since he apparently has a stronger
sex drive than the female, is more compelled to
select a mate than is she. The male, then, is the
aggressor. As Barash (1977:146) puts it:

In most vertebrate animals, the role of
advertiser is performed by the male,
while the female is the discriminating

26

customer. Males tend to be selected for salesmanship; females for sales resistance. The reason for this distinction goes to the heart of male-female differences and is crucial to an understanding of the sociobiology of courtship and mate selection.

It is obvious, then, that males and females have very different roles, which are genetically determined. The male courts the female and becomes more aggressive and violent, both for purposes of courtship and in order to provide food and protection for the female and the infant. It is the woman's role to provide milk, warmth, and love to the child; and also to provide sexual activity to the male. These two tasks are not always compatible (LaBarre, 1955:123): ". . . the human female is at once the necessary oral object of the infant and the genital object of the male--her body, so to speak, the battleground of divergent biological interests." The resolution of this battle, however, makes the family possible. LaBarre continues (p.124): "The child possesses the breast, the father the sexuality, of the mother: on this biological bargain the family is founded."

The formation of the family unit in this fashion is extremely important because, LaBarre argues (p.210), "The family is not a creation of culture; without the family there would be no culture!" Human culture brings with it language, learning, and the ability to manipulate symbols. But what is the relationship between this ultimate achievement of humans and the biological imperative which makes it possible? For LaBarre as for Freud, one thing that happens is that culture can come into opposition to man's nature (p.33): "Only a few human societies, and at their peril, have culturally invaded the ancient mammalian adjustment of mother and her child." Tiger and Shepher (1975) argue, in support of this statement, that cultural attempts to alter this innate mother-child bond such as have occurred in the Kibbutz, are doomed to failure.

27

The purpose of being human, according to LaBarre (p.109), is to procreate in a family context:

> . . . the full adult social state in all societies is a procreative membership in a biological family--not necessarily monogamous . . . not necessarily lifelong in duration, but nevertheless a condition toward which all adult humans permanently strive.

Culture, however, can threaten this drive as well, and cause people to misconstrue their true purpose (p.106): "It is a tragedy of our male-centered culture that women do not fully enough know how important they are as women." Apparently, women who see the central role in their lives as being anything other than to provide sex to her mate and love and nourishment to her children is a threat to society as well as to herself. However, even women's liberation will not destroy us because, LaBarre says (p.106): "Luckily, there are always enough women who respect themselves to serve as models for those who do not."

Other kinds of mischief can threaten our biological natures as a result of culture. LaBarre argues (p.218):

> The biologist is forced to conclude that behavior which is non-adaptive biologically, but only adaptive psychologically, is properly not his concern but the psychiatrist's; that homosexuality among humans is not a genuine variety of love but a dishonest and desperate neurotic game, arising from unsuccess in escaping from the family-of-origin to a family-of-procreation.

LaBarre's own obvious contempt for homosexuality itself, he argues, is justified genetically, (p.103) since:

. . . submission as a homosexual object
is implicated with inferiority in the
infrahuman primate this is probably the
phylogenetic root of man's conscious,
ineradicable recognition of homosexuality
as a biological deficiency.

Since the purpose of sexuality is to repro-
duce in a family setting, any sexuality which is
not directed toward that end fails to be biologi-
cally adaptive, and is wrong. This is especially
true for women; they seem not to have the same
kind of strong sex drive as men and must follow
their biological dictates to hold the family together. The men have less natural attachment to
the family. This produces a double standard. Sex
outside the confines of the family is definitely
maladaptive (wrong) for women; promiscuity for men,
on the other hand, is understandable if not totally acceptable. According to LaBarre (p.62),
". . . in human males there is extraordinarily
great variability in sexual activity." The desire
for men to mate with virgins who thereafter remain
faithful may also be genetically determined.
Barash (1977:152) argues, in a discussion of the
mating habits of species "requiring considerable
parental care in the rearing of offspring . . ."
that ". . . they behaved in accordance with sociobiologic theory in that they were disinclined to
mate with females who had already been involved
with other males." Furthermore, he continues,
"There may be parallels here in human behavior,
whether reflecting cultural practices or evolutionary wisdom."

Sociobiology, then, sanctions social systems
which control or repress their sexuality, but
leaves room for a double standard. Sociological
functionalism comes to much the same conclusion,
but argues from the position of sociological,
rather than biological, requirements.

A functionalist begins an analysis of society
by determining what the primary goals and objec-
tives of that society are, then determines whether

29

the particular traits or practices of that society are helpful (functional) or destructive (disfunctional) to those basic goals. Society is seen as a mechanism which strives to maintain stasis and functional relatedness of its separate parts. Anything which threatens this balance is dangerous and therefore "bad."

The functionalist in the United States falls roughly into the control-repression model, which in turn is regarded as being conservative by many. This bias is not an inherent characteristic of functionalism, however. As Gouldner (1970) points out, functionalists are not inherently conservative in the conservative vs. liberal sense, but are conservative in the sense that they support the status quo in the system of which they are a part. To put it another way, the functionalists can always be found riding carefully on the mode of their society's bell curve of values. So when we put the functionalists into a control-repression model, that is one indication that it is the dominant model of society.

The functionalists arrive at their positions in a different way from those of either the traditional or Freudian repressionists, and in some respects are less rigid in their prescriptions; but there are many similarities. People who differ from the dominant morality of their society are not sinful, neurotic, sick, or perverted; they are deviants. Changes which threaten the social order are not heathen or Satanic; they represent social disorganization.

Kingsley Davis is a functionalist who writes about sexual behavior; it is essentially his position which will be used here to describe the sociological control-repression model. (All quotes from Davis, 1971, unless otherwise noted.) Davis admits that sexual activities, like other human behavior, need to be learned; but he does not follow this statement to its logical conclusions as the learning theorists do. Instead he moves immediately to a nearly Freudian view (p.315):

>As a powerful drive, sex can be utilized
>to motivate people to perform in ways that
>benefit the community at large, while lack
>of regulation may bring conflict and
>disruption.

The two major institutions which this regulation
serves are the family and the exchange system.
Davis points out that all known societies exert
some control over sexuality. The controls may
vary from one society to the next, but they all
support the marriage and family structure of which
they are a part.

The sex norms which cannot be explained by
reference to the family system can generally be
explained in the context of the need to supply the
goods and services. Davis (p.321) notes:

>Since sexual desirability is itself a
>good, sexual access can be exchanged for
>economic or political advantage. The
>distribution of sexual favors thus gets
>involved with the distribution of politi-
>cal and economic goods.

(See the reference to the capitalist metaphor
above.) This kind of apparently objective analysis seems, in the hands of the functionalists, to
move rapidly from description to prescription. It
is but a short jump from "If adultery is wide-
spread, it will destroy the current family structure" to "We must not permit adultery." This sort
of jump seems to occur frequently as Davis dis-
cusses various "deviant" sexual practices. It may
be true, too, that with the functionalists as well
as the authors of the Bible, people act on inter-
pretations that may or may not be accurate perceptions of what was meant. If this is the case, the
comment made with reference to the Bible is relevant here: it is what people believe to be true
that dictates their actions, and that is what is
important for our purposes here.

31

Davis's discussion of premarital sexual relations will be our first case in point. Although
many societies formally ban premarital sex, seldom is the ban entirely effective. It is seldom
enforced with the same strength as certain other
deviations. Why might this be true? Davis (p.330)
tells us:

> premarital sex is widely debated be-
> cause its regulation is less fundamen-
> tal than the regulation of many other
> aspects of sexual life. In other words,
> the premarital rules are marginal; they
> can be one way or the other without
> altering the character of the society.

In spite of this relative unimportance of the
norms governing premarital sex, Davis (p.334)
expresses concern over the rising rates of this
activity in contemporary society:

> The rise in premarital coitus is often
> attributed to a change in moral
> standards, but one can argue just as
> well that it is due to a breakdown of
> standards, and that until new ones
> arise, the situation is one of disor-
> ganization rather than reorganization.
> If reorganization does occur, it will
> doubtless be because of the problems
> created by the present condition.

Notice that the "problem" is with the illicit
activity, not the ban on it; and the problem will
lead to "disorganization" which is generally considered to be bad.

Davis (p.334) indicates that one problem
which arises from premarital coitus is that the
woman is giving up her bargaining power:

> Formerly in northwest European society
> a respectable woman gave her sexual
> favors only in return for the promise
> of a stable relationship and economic

support. The man was drawn into the
bargain by his sexual interest. If he
obtained coitus under false pretenses,
he risked retaliation by the girl's
relatives and loss of face. The girl
could thus use her relatively short
period of maximum attractiveness to
settle her future in the best way pos-
sible--by marriage.

But now, with increasing rates of premarital sex,
the woman is giving away what she could once have
been compensated for. This quote also contains
some assumptions about the nature of sexuality:
the man has the stronger sex drive, so women
would apparently not want to engage in sex simply
for pleasure or release of sex drive; women seem
to have no assets other than sexual attractiveness to use for bargaining power; the bargaining
power decreases once virginity is lost; the ultimate goal for women is marriage; and beauty is
inherently more prevalent in young people. There
are some people who would take issue with one or
more of these assumptions.

Unwise bargaining is not the only outcome of
premarital sex; there are several other possi-
bilities, as Davis (p.336) informs us:
"Unmarried coitus can have one or more of several
outcomes: nothing at all beyond the act itself,
venereal disease, an illicit pregnancy ending in
abortion, a forced marriage, or an illegitimate
child." With four out of five of his possibili-
ties being negative, it is not surprising that he
concludes (p.340):

All told, the hazards of premarital intercourse are not slight.
For the woman, they seem to outweigh
the advantages. At least under the old
system there was a sense of a fair bargain. Under contemporary conditions,
there is hardly any system of premarital conduct; it is each for himself.
Many get hurt.

Having disposed of the problem of premarital coitus, Davis then turns his attention to prostitution. He notes that it exists in many societies and, with a few exceptions such as temple prostitution, is generally frowned on. The reason given for this is a good example of functionalist thought (p.341):

> Prostitution is officially condemned in contemporary industrial societies mainly because it fulfills no recognized goal. The norms of every society tend to link the sexual act to some stable, or potentially stable, social relationship.

But prostitution still exists and laws against it are difficult to enforce. This, too, has a functional explanation (p.345):

> . . . when prostitution is outlawed, it falls into a category of crime that is notoriously hard to control--the type in which one of the guilty parties is the ordinary law-abiding citizen, who is receiving an illicit service. It is economically and politically foolish to punish a large number of a society's productive and otherwise orderly members.

Other kinds of analyses might raise issues of fairness of the criminal justice system or unequal distribution of power.

Functional analyses of prostitution have been around a long time. The ancient Romans Ovid and Cicero defended prostitution on the grounds that it allowed men the opportunity to release their powerful sex drive in a context which would be unlikely to lead to any emotional attachment. It would, therefore, be less threatening to the family than the alternative of adultery. The Hebrew discussion of prostitution (see above) has a similar ring.

Davis (p.354) also disapproves of homosexuality

because it "is obviously incompatible with the family and the sexual bargaining system." Since homosexuality is disfunctional, its attraction must be a negative rather than positive one (p.356): "The homosexual's problem is not so much that he is attracted to males, but that he is in flight from females." Also since it is disfunctional (p.359):

> . . . homosexual behavior gives rise to problems considered serious in modern times. Among these, homosexual prostitution, venereal disease, crime, and youth corruption are the most important. . . . Apart from robbery and violence associated with male prostitution, the main hazards of homosexual conduct are blackmail, homicidal jealousy, and marital fraud.

Perhaps the major reason that homosexuality is so widely disapproved is the one given so often by Anita Bryant but quoted here from Kingsley Davis (p.360): "The homosexual group . . . is preeminently one in which membership is by re-cruitment (seduction), and it will die out without it."

The sociological control-repression model might best be summarized by this last quote from Davis (p.359): "Our analysis has shown . . . that sexual norms reflect sociological requirements." In other words, if the norm exists it is important to the survival of society. It is "right" and should not be violated. "Normal" sexual behavior does not need to be explained; it is either natural or socially necessary or both. Only the "deviant" behavior needs to be explained and dealt with.

The implications for social control of the sociological control-repression model, then, are very similar to those of traditional and Freudian control-repression models. One area of possible disagreement might be on the topic of birth

control. Contraception might be seen to be functional in the light of the current population
explosion. Prohibitions against birth control are
an example of "cultural survivals"--traits which
were at one time functional, but still exist in a
society where their functions have been lost.
However, Davis notes that it is precisely in this
age of widely available birth control that we are
experiencing a tremendous increase in venereal
disease, abortion, illegitimate births, divorce,
and adultery. Whether he assumes a causal relationship to all these disfunctional consequences
is not fully spelled out.

THE NATURAL EXPRESSION MODELS

The natural expression models have a long history in Western thought. They can be traced back to Plato, who advocated pederasty as a pure, natural form of sexual expression. In the more modern sense, precursors of the model begin to appear roughly around the time of the American revolution: Mary Wollstonecraft, William Godwin, Charles Brockden Brown, and others. The nineteenth century produced "free-lovers" including Moses Harmon, Edwin Walker, the Chaflin sisters (Tennie and Victoria) and many others (cf. Ditzion, 1969). The discussion here will limit itself to the most prominent twentieth century proponents of this view.

Although Freud was the father of a control-repression model, there is the seed in his works for a far different approach. One of his major contributions was to the legitimization of talk about sex, first among psychoanalytic practitioners and then among the general population. Some of his followers became more repressive than he himself was, but others took the opportunity to lend the weight of science to the support of people who were beginning to rebel against the repressiveness of Puritanism and Victorianism.

Social conditions were very different from those which existed at the time the Bible was written and codified. Industrialization and urbanization were rapidly occurring, loosening family and community ties. The individualism which was spurred by Luther and Calvin was turning on its fathers to weaken the very morality they proposed. Changes in morality found their champions in writers like Wilhelm Reich and Rene Guyon. The debate had long been gathering momentum, but these and many others provided legitimacy to the rebellion against control-repressionism.

37

The sex expression models agree with the control-repressionists that there is such a thing as a strong sex drive. But the expressionists believe that the drive is natural, good, and should not be repressed. The form that the various theorists thought natural expression would take constitutes the major differences between the nature-limited expression and the natural diverse expression models.

The Nature-Limited Expression Model

Wilhelm Reich, a younger contemporary of Freud, is the major proponent of this model. Among his major works are The Mass Psychology of Fascism (1933) and The Function of the Orgasm (1942). The latter work came out in two volumes, the first of which was The Discovery of Orgone. The second, The Cancer Biopathy, was banned and burned by the Food and Drug Administration, the only book ever burned by agents of the United States government. Before being arrested in the United States for his work (by the F.B.I. in 1941), he was expelled from the Freudian-dominated International Psychoanalytic Association (1934); left Germany under threat of his life; and was harassed in Norway (1938). He died in an American jail in 1956 while serving a two-year sentence for treating cancer patients with his orgone accumulator (Popenoe, 1976). His knowledge of sex can be questioned. His understanding of Fascism cannot.

Reich constantly acknowledged his debt to Freud who, Reich felt, was essentially correct but did not go far enough. Freud's major problem was that he did not have an anthropological perspective. He wrote about the Austrian personality as though it were the only possibility. He was right, then, in assuming that repression is necessary for civilization if by civilization one means patriarchal and authoritarian civilization. It is precisely this kind of civilization which is the most repressive, and that is why Freud saw the personality structure in the way that he did.

Reich (1942:204) describes this type of personality structure:

> The patriarchal, authoritarian era in human history has attempted to keep the secondary antisocial drives in check with the aid of compulsive moral restrictions. Thus, what is called the cultured human came to be a living structure composed of three layers. On the surface he carries the artificial mask of self-control, of compulsive, insincere politeness and of artificial sociality. With this layer, he covers up the second one, the Freudian "unconscious" in which sadism, greediness, lasciviousness, envy, perversions of all kinds, etc., are kept in check, without however having in the least lost any of their power. The second layer is the artifact of a sex-negating culture; consciously, it is mostly experienced only as a gaping inner emptiness. Behind it, in the depths, live and work natural sociality and sexuality, spontaneous enjoyment of work, capacity for love. This third and deepest layer, representing the biological nucleus of the human structure, is unconscious and dreaded. It is at variance with every aspect of authoritarian education and regime. It is, at the same time, man's only real hope of ever mastering social misery.

Reich turns Freud upside down. It is not repression which results in higher cultural achievements; it is repression which prevents higher cultural achievements. Repression has disastrous effects not only on civilization but on the individual's personality and body as well.

Reich replaces Freud's notion of libidinal energy with his own concept of orgone energy. Nor is orgone energy simply a hypothetical construct, as is libidinal energy. Orgone energy is biological and measurable. Reich (1942:361) defines it in his glossary this way:

> Orgone Energy. Primordial Cosmic Energy;
> universally present and demonstrable visu-
> ally, thermically, electroscopically and
> by means of Geiger-Mueller counters. In
> the living organism: Bio-energy, Life
> Energy.

Orgone energy exists in all matter, both organic
and inorganic. In the individual human, it takes
the form of genital energy.

In the patriarchal, authoritarian society this
energy is constantly being repressed, beginning in
infancy (1942:78):

> In the first phase, much harm is done
> by strict and premature training for excre-
> mental cleanliness, and the demands to be
> "good," to show absolute self-restraint
> and quiet good behavior. These measures
> prepare the ground for the most important
> prohibitions of the following period, the
> prohibition of masturbation. Other re-
> strictions of infantile development may
> vary but these are typical. The inhibi-
> tion of infantile sexuality is the basis
> for the fixation to the parental home and
> its atmosphere, the "family." This is the
> origin of the typical lack of independence
> in thought and action. Psychic mobility
> and strength go with sexual mobility and
> cannot exist without it. Conversely,
> psychic inhibition and awkwardness pre-
> supposes sexual inhibition.

Reich feels that the latency period proposed by
Freud is not natural but is the result of repression. In adolescence, Reich says (1942:253),
repression does have the effect of "making the
adolescent submissive and capable of marriage.
. . . But in doing so it creates the very sexual
impotence which in turn destroys marriage and
accentuates the problem of marriage."

One effect this constant repression of orgone can have is to make the individual aggressive. Freud proposed, at various times, the death instinct and the aggressive instinct to account for human destructiveness. As an instinct, then, it had to be repressed. Reich (1942:131) had a different view:

> The goal of aggression is always that of making possible the gratification of a vital need. Aggression is, therefore, not an instinct in the proper sense, but the indispensable means of gratifying any instinct. The instinct in itself is aggressive because the tension calls for gratification.

The effect of expression rather than repression, then, would be to get rid of aggression, not to cause it. This is a key break from Freud. It demonstrates Reich's essentially optimistic view of human nature as against Freud's pessimism.

Repression has disastrous effects on the human body as well. It could result in many illnesses, including heart trouble ("cardiac anxiety") and cancer. To discuss these would necessitate explanation of his biological analysis of orgone, which would take us beyond the purpose of this paper. Suffice it to say that it was his thesis that an expressive sex life could prevent, and orgone treatment cure, cancer; it was this view that got him into trouble with the Food and Drug Administration. It is ironic that Freud had cancer and died in exile from his native country, while Reich, also an exile, died while in jail for trying to treat cancer. At any rate, Reich is often seen as a precursor of contemporary bioenergetics research (Popenoe, 1976).

In his psychiatric practice, Reich had ample opportunity to study the effect of repression on individuals. His observations led him (1942:93) to conclude that "The severity of any kind of psychic disturbance is in direct relation to the

41

severity of the disturbance of genitality." It was, therefore, obvious that "The prognosis depends directly on the possibility of establishing the capacity for full genital satisfaction." The goal, then, was to establish "orgastic potency" which is described (1942:79) as the

> capacity for surrender to the flow of biological energy without any inhibition, the capacity for complete discharge of all dammed-up sexual excitation through involuntary pleasurable contractions of the body. . . . The intensity of pleasure in the orgasm (in the sexual act which is free of anxiety and unpleasure, and unaccompanied by phantasies) depends on the amount of sexual tension concentrated in the genitals; the pleasure is all the more intense the greater in amount and the steeper the "drop" in the excitation.

For the male, ejaculation did not necessarily indicate full orgastic potency. It is possible to ejaculate without experiencing the full pleasure which should result from orgasm. Although Reich had an extremely detailed account of the phases of sexual excitement, quite similar to those later described by Masters and Johnson (1966), he perpetuated Freud's distinction between the clitoral and vaginal orgasm in women. He was right, however, when he was one of the first researchers to believe that a full orgasm would be much the same in men and women.

The individual could become fully orgastic through psychotherapy and the proper application of "sex economy" which was defined (1942:361) as: "The body of knowledge within Orgonomy which deals with the economy of the biological (orgone) energy in the organism, with its energy household."

Reich, during the rise of Hitler, gradually began to see the futility of dealing with individuals one at a time in psychotherapy. The

42

entire society was going mad. In his (1951:xix) estimation, "90% of all novels and 99% of all films and plays are productions whose appeal is to unsatisfied sexual needs." What was even more terrifying was his (1942:135) diagnosis that nearly the entire population was neurotic or worse:

> . . . in the case of an organization for sex hygiene embracing the whole population at best 30% of the people could be helped by simple measures. The rest of the population, i.e. about 70% (more in women, less in men), needed intensive therapy, requiring in each case--with a doubtful outcome--an average of two or three years. To set oneself such a goal for one's practical social endeavor was senseless. Mental hygiene on such an individualistic basis was nothing but a dangerous utopia.

The figures seem ridiculously high--it was only a small minority who were "normal." But considering the fact that these estimates were made in Germany in the early 1930's, his guesses seem, in retrospect, to be remarkably accurate.

The cause of these individual repressions was the rise of the Great Repression, Fascism; and the cause of Fascism was all these individual repressions. Reich (1951:37) did not blame Fascism totally on Hitler: "What is new in Fascism is that the masses of people themselves assented to their own subjugation and actively brought it about." The masses, not realizing that the freedom and fulfillment they desired could only come through developing orgastic potential, believed in a man who promised to deliver through other means. Hitler was appealing, though in a mystical way, to deeply vital forces. The masses had, through repression, been well prepared. They had been trained to give in to the patriarch; they had been trained to submit to the state; they had been trained to be obedient to religion; they had learned race pride and racial hatred. When an abortive attempt at "democracy" failed, they turned in the direction for which they had been prepared--total submission to an all-powerful authority. It was no accident that sexual freedom was one of the first things Hitler attacked.

Reich (1942:218) proposed, by way of counter-offensive, to mount a massive movement to teach the principles of orgasmic potential:

> The only way of combatting the pathological sexuality which forms the fertile soil for Hitler's theory of race and for Streicher's criminal activity is to contrast it to the natural sexual processes and attitudes. The people will immediately grasp the difference and will show burning interest in it, once they are shown what it is that they really want and only do not dare to express.

This massive educational program would proceed through the distribution of handbills and through speeches and seminars. As we know, it met with no success. The masses had had their first doses of Fascism, and were already addicted.

Reich was not just fighting against Fascism; he was fighting for an expressive society, and he had an image of what it would be like. He had noticed that some of the people who had developed orgastic potential through his sex-economic psychoanalysis had found themselves unable to return to their work. This would seem to validate Freud's hypothesis that work resulted from sublimation of libido. But on further analysis, Reich discovered that it was only the dull, monotonous, alienating kinds of jobs that the potent person could not do. Those who had jobs which were personally rewarding, creative, and fulfilling were able to work even better after becoming orgastically potent. The nonrepressive society, then, would be without repressive jobs; it would be what Reich (1942:xxiv) called a "work democracy":

The age-old, genuine striving for a
democratization of social life is based
on self-determination, on natural
sociality and morality, on joyful work
and earthly happiness in love. People
with this striving consider any illusion
a danger. Thus, they will not only be
unafraid of the scientific comprehension
of the living function, but they will put
it to use in mastering decisive problems
pertaining to the formation of human
character structure; in so doing, they
will be able to master these problems
in a scientific and practical, instead
of in an illusionary manner. Everywhere
people are striving to turn formal democracy into a true democracy of all those
engaged in productive work, into a work
democracy, that is, a democracy on the
basis of a natural organization of the
work process.

The nonrepressive society would, of course,
be different also in terms of its sexual relationships; but social changes would have to come first
(1951:119): "The social prerequisites of the
lasting sexual relationship would be economic in-
dependence of the woman, social care and education
of the children, lack of interference by economic
interests." Equality for women is essential if
women as well as men are to be free to form relationships based on love and sexual attraction
rather than financial necessity.

Natural expression of sexuality would, however, not lead to a "permissive" society, but to
more or less long-lasting relationships. The
promiscuous person in the repressive society is
continually searching for true orgastic potential,
but never finds it. Full orgastic potency com-
bined tenderness, caring, and a full knowledge of
the partner. This can only reach its fullest
expression in a long-lasting relationship.

The young will, of course, masturbate.

Adolescents will often have several sexual partners, but usually consecutively rather than
simultaneously. Homosexuality will not frequently
occur; not because there will be laws against it,
but because it is an aberration caused by repression. Although sexual relationships will tend to
be long-lasting, they will not be of the lifelong
"for better or for worse" variety imposed by traditional marriage in the repressive society.
Spouses may have an occasional sexual encounter
outside the marriage. If they do, one of two
things will happen. More likely than not, they
will find the encounter unfulfilling and will return to the established relationship. Occasion-
ally, they will find the new relationship more
pleasurable, and will break off the old relationship. This may cause some jealousy and pain; but
the freedom to create new relationships when the
old one has faded causes much less pain than
being compelled to stay in the old, unsatisfying
marriage. It is because Reich feels that the
natural expression of sexuality would lead to
relatively long-lasting heterosexual relationships
that his views would fit the nature-limiting
expression model.

Reich's concern with repression and alienation has made his views compatible in some respect
with Marxism; at least he has been interpreted in
that way by later readers. He himself, however,
was careful to point out the differences between
his views and at least what he saw as "vulgar"
Marxism. Reich (1933:xx) takes issue with sim-
plistic definitions of class:

> In the Marxism of the 19th century,
> "class consciousness" was limited to the
> manual workers. The other working people
> in vitally necessary professions, without
> which society could not function, were
> distinguished from this "proletariat" as
> "intellectuals" and "petit-bourgeois."
> This schematic and obsolete distinction
> was a major contributing factor in the
> victory of fascism in Germany. The

46

concept of "class consciousness" is not
only too narrow; it does not even corre-
spond to the structure of the class of
manual workers. "Industrial work" and
"proletarian" are, therefore, replaced by
the concepts of "vitally necessary work"
and the "working individual." These two
concepts comprise all who do socially
vital work, that is, in addition to the
industrial workers, the physicians,
teachers, technicians, laboratory workers,
writers, social administrators, farmers,
scientific workers, etc. This eliminates
a chasm which has done much to disrupt
working human society and thus has contributed to fascism, be it the black or
red variety.

Marxist sociology, out of its ig-
norance of mass psychology, contrasted
the "bourgeois" with the "proletarian."
This is erroneous. A certain character
structure is not limited to the capitalist,
but pervades the working people in all
professions. There are revolutionary
capitalists and reactionary workers.
There are no characterological class
distinctions in the biophysical depth
of human structure.

Reich further develops his concept of class in his
1944 preface to The Sexual Revolution (p.xii):

The social concepts of the 19th century,
with their purely economic definition,
no longer apply to the ideological
stratification we see in the cultural
struggles of the 20th century. The
social struggles of today, to reduce it
to the simplest formula, are between the
interests safeguarding and affirming life
on the one hand, and the interests
destroying and suppressing life on the
other. The basic social question is no
longer, "Are you rich or poor?" It is:

47

"Do you favor, and do you fight for, the
safeguarding of and the greatest possible
freedom of human life? Do you do, in a
practical way, everything in your power
to make the masses of working individuals
so independent in their thinking, acting,
and living that the complete self-
regulation of human life will become a
matter of course in a not too distant
future?"

This theme is picked up by Herbert Marcuse,
who combines neo-Freudianism and neo-Marxism in an
attack on modern repressive society. In the tech-
nological society, the sex instinct falls into the
use of the reality principle. This creates the
ethic of productivity which demands that people
become machine-like extensions of the producing
society. The pleasure principle is repressed in
the service of production. In this utilitarian
society, the sex instinct is to be directed only
towards procreation, for this is the only "productive" use of it. The sexual perversions arise
as an unconscious rebellion to the alienated
labor which results from the ethic of production
and efficiency. In the nonrepressive society, the
rebellion would not be necessary, so only "natural"
sex would occur.

The dehumanizing aspects of contemporary
society have been pointed out by a number of other
writers, including Rollo May. He feels that many
of the people who think they have been sexually
liberated are actually as repressed as their Victorian predecessors. The emphasis on technique in
sex; the use of sex in advertising; the obligatory
sex scenes in novels and movies; the Playboy ethic;
all these are dehumanizing and repressive. There
is in contemporary society a new puritanism, which
consists of three elements (May, 1969:45): "First,
a state of alienation from the body. Second, the
separation of emotion from reason. And third, the
use of the body as a machine." He (1969:47) calls
this person who feels enlightened and nonrepressed

the "new sophisticate" and draws this impression-
istic sketch:

> The new sophisticate is not castrated
> by society, but like Origen is self cas-
> trated. Sex and the body are for him not
> something to be and live out, but tools
> to be cultivated like a T.V. announcer's
> voice. The new sophisticate expresses
> his passion by devoting himself passion-
> ately to the moral principle of dispersing
> all passion, loving everybody until love
> has no power left to scare anyone. He is
> deathly afraid of his passions unless they
> are kept under leash, and the theory of
> total expression is precisely his leash.
> His dogma of liberty is his repression;
> and his principle of full libidinal health,
> full sexual satisfaction, is his denial
> of eros. The old Puritans repressed sex
> and were passionate; our new puritan re-
> presses passion and is sexual. His pur-
> pose is to hold back the body, to try to
> make nature a slave. The new sophisti-
> cate's rigid principle of full freedom is
> not freedom but a new straitjacket. He
> does all this because he is afraid of his
> body and his compassionate roots in na-
> ture, afraid of the soil and his pro-
> creative power. He is our latter-day
> Baconian devoted to gaining power over
> nature, gaining knowledge in order to get
> more power. And you gain power over
> sexuality (like working the slave until
> all zest for revolt is squeezed out of
> him) precisely by the role of full expres-
> sion. Sex becomes our tool like the cave-
> man's bow and arrows, crowbar, or adz.
> Sex, the new machine, the Machina Ultima.

May, like Reich, would not necessarily prescribe
laws against this dehumanizing sex, but obviously
feels that naturally expressed sexuality would be
of a far different kind than this. This is the
essence of the nature-limited expressionist model.

The Natural Diverse Expression Model

Instead of believing that a nonrepressive sexual atmosphere would result in rather limited forms of sexual expression, writers like Rene Guyon expected natural expression to result in very diverse manifestations of the sex drive. Guyon was a widely traveled French lawyer who, in 1919, became a judge in the Supreme Court of Siam. It was while he was there that he wrote his two major works: The Ethics of Sexual Acts, 1930; and Sexual Freedom, 1939. While his views were similar to those of Reich in many ways, there is no indication that they were aware of each other's work. Neither cites the other in their respective books.

Guyon claimed to be a rationalist; his works include perspectives from anthropology, the natural sciences, natural law, and Freud. While Reich complained that Freud did not go far enough in failing to see that repression was only necessary in the patriarchal-authoritarian society, Guyon felt that Freud went too far in believing that repression was ever necessary. Guyon (1930:27) summarizes what he considers the crucial doctrines of Freud:

(a) The sexual emotions and desires play an important and continuous role in the individual mind.

(b) This is true even in the case of children.

(c) The institution of the "Censor," which represses these sexual desires, and drives back into the unconscious all ideas associated with them (ideas which our modern morals regard as wicked and shameful), is due ultimately to the antisexual bias imported to the growing mind by our social system.

(d) Repression is a condition which

is responsible for the formation of the symptoms which reveal the presence of a neurosis due to the nonsatisfaction of sexual needs; these symptoms are in the nature of a pis-aller or a defence; "human beings become neurotic when they are prevented from satisfying their libido."

(e) When the watchfulness which an individual exercises on himself is relaxed for any reason, the repressed sexual manifestations begin to appear and reveal their importance in a more or less coherent manner (i.e. dreams, delirium, and anxiety).

The notion of infant sexuality is an important one for Guyon. It helped prove that (1930:10) "the human being has no need to be taught how to use his sexual organs for their immediate purpose, which is that of giving pleasure." Sexual expression, then, is natural; but more important than that, its purpose in providing pleasure is separate from its function of reproduction (1930:72):

There exists in the child, from the first years onwards and well before any possibility of copulation or of reproduction, a diffused and attenuated sexual pleasure sui generis; and this pleasure is manifested in the overwhelming attraction exercised by the sexual organs, and in the great satisfaction occasioned by their stimulation in any form, either individually or with other persons.

Guyon was taking issue here with the traditional moralities which proclaimed that the only proper purpose for sexual activity was reproduction, and then only in the confines of marriage. He cites other examples to prove his point. Not only does sexual enjoyment begin in infancy, but it extends into old age, far beyond the end of reproductive capability. Also, only a tiny

51

minority of the acts of coitus result in conception. Reich (1942:175) also made this point:

> Biologically speaking, the healthy human organism calls for three to four thousand sexual acts in the course of a genital life of, say, 30 to 40 years. The wish for offspring is satisfied with two to four children. Moralistic and ascetic ideologies condone sexual pleasure even in marriage only for the purpose of procreation; carried to its logical conclusion, that would mean at the most four sexual acts in a lifetime.

The reverse, continues Guyon (1930:82), is also true; reproduction can occur without coitus:

> . . . it suffices to bring the male fluid into contact with the ovules of the female to obtain reproduction, and this can occur without intromission of the penis, nay, even without contact of any kind between the male and the female.

Even pleasure is not, at least on the part of the woman, necessary for conception. In addition, sexual pleasure can result from coitus while the woman is pregnant, when it could have no possible procreative purpose. Finally, sexual pleasure often occurs without heterosexual contact, as in masturbation and homosexuality.

Natural sexual pleasure, then, can be totally separated from its reproductive function. It is many-sided, like that which occurs in the infant; what Freud called "polymorphous-perverse." Natural sexual expression is the same in the adult as in the child; any form of it is proper. Incest desires, for example, occur naturally in the child. It is only the jealousy of the boy's father (or the girl's mother) and our outmoded sense of morality which prevent the full expression of incest. There is no natural incest taboo, as the story of Oedipus itself indicates. Jocasta and Oedipus enjoyed their sexual relationship until their biological relationship came to light. Even then Jocasta tried to keep the truth from Oedipus so that their marriage could continue. It was the social definition of the relationship, not the biological relationship itself, which caused the problem.

Nothing is naturally wrong, either, with exhibitionism. We are born naked; it is only outmoded morality (and perhaps, one might add, inclement weather) which dictates that we wear clothes. Besides, it is only the hopelessly repressed individual who is really offended by it. Nor is it a sign of total moral depravity; Diogenes masturbated in crowds so that others might follow his example.

Some homosexuality, says Guyon, is physiologically determined and therefore natural for those people. For others it is a temporary expediency in the absence of a member of the opposite sex; for still others it is simply a matter of personal preference. Whatever its cause, it undoubtedly results in pleasure for those who engage in it, and is therefore not a perversion but another example of the diversity of natural sexual activity. Necrophilia is not a perversion either; it is ordinarily only an occasional practice, and usually ceases when the subject begins to enjoy a normal sex life. Coprophilia, too, is simply a matter of taste; after all, "some people like to eat Munster and Livarot cheese." Neither bestiality nor fetishism are perversions either, for the same reasons.

Sadism presents a somewhat different picture. It is not solely a sexual act--it is also a violent one. Since sexuality is not to be judged wrong, "sadism is to be judged blameworthy to exactly the same extent that cruelty--which is an integral part of it--is blameworthy." Since masochism only harms the self, it should be outside the reach of social sanctions: ". . . in essence it seems to belong to those classes of preference which, in virtue of

53

their purely personal character, are of no interest from the point of view of general ethics." Guyon (1930:344) proposes the following principles:

> (i) It is wrong to suppose that ordinary coitus is the only normal mode of <u>sexual satisfaction</u>; it is the only normal mode of <u>reproduction</u>, but that is quite a different thing.

> (ii) Every mechanical means of producing sexual pleasure is normal and legitimate; there is no room for moral distinctions between the various available methods; all are equally justifiable and equally suited to their particular ends.

> (iii) The personal characteristics of the sexual partner have nothing to do with the physiological manifestations of sexual pleasure itself; the importance attributed to these characteristics is a matter of convention, and varies from age to age; indeed, even though the personality of the partner were totally unknown, this would make no difference to the sexual act, the specific pleasure of which would remain completely unaffected.

Sexual pleasure is natural and good. Moralities, Guyon (1930:113) feels, are something else:

> . . . the moral elements in sex are all creations of the human mind which have been superimposed upon the original physiological facts. They have no basis in these facts themselves. This morality is made up of <u>convention</u>, i.e., an understanding between certain human beings to interpret the physiological facts in a certain way.

The further a morality deviates from natural law, the worse it is; and the Judeo-Christian and Victorian moralities are quite bad. They result in repression which, in turn, has some disastrous consequences. Freud found that repression was the principal cause of neuroses which can, in some cases, be quite severe. Guyon (1939:9) guesses that "'Jack the Ripper' was probably a purity-fanatic run mad." He also indicates that in America, where repression is probably the most severe, one also finds the highest rates of crime and drug use. Natural expression of sex will result in lower rates of crime, less use of intoxicants, and less personal neurosis. In fact, these things might be eliminated. Obviously, an attack on the traditional moralities is called for.

One group which should be leading this reform are psychiatrists; instead they themselves have become an oppressive force. Although he stops short of accusing psychiatry of creating mental illness, as have more recent writers like Szasz, Guyon (1930:26) does see complicity between psychiatry and the dominant order:

> Influenced by a thousand obscure and unavowed motives, psychiatry has sided with the social conventions, and has therefore inevitably changed the natural roles, reversed the usual terminology of medicine, and looked upon those who do not conform to the conventional rules as being abnormal and therefore pathological. . . . As between nature and convention, psychiatry always sides with convention, and brands the natural as "the abnormal." Starting from this disloyalty to its own scientific premises, psychiatry soon becomes blind to all logical conclusions.

Guyon (1939:136-7) combines his views with what he calls a positive program in this statement:

> 1. Sexual freedom must be provided with a rock-bottom foundation by a deliberate adhesion to the doctrine and the principles of the legitimacy of sexual

acts, this implying the conquest of repression and the censorship.

2. We must apply to sexual acts the principles of the mechanistic theory; that is to say, the idea that the sexual object does not form a necessary part of the appreciation or performance of a sexual act, every mechanical realisation being a sufficient end in itself.

3. We must never admit that sexual relations are blameworthy, so long as they do not imply the use of force upon a non-consenting party. On the contrary, we must assure ourselves and others that sexual acts are fully legitimate and perfectly avowable, that there is nothing immoral or shameful about them, and that they are entirely compatible with human dignity, which can never be impaired by the fulfillment of natural law. To affirm sexual need is no more ridiculous than to affirm chastity, being equally honourable.

4. We must strenuously contest the idea that there can be anything degrading in having freely performed a sexual act.

5. We must unhesitatingly be prepared to perform sexual acts with due deference to the rights of others . . . , their only purpose being to secure one of the most desirable, most refined, and most legitimate of human pleasures, and one which is an end in itself. Nor must we ever consider the offer of or the demand for a sexual act as offensive, for it is a compliment.

6. By our behavior and in our speech we should ensure that sexual manifestations shall become as much a matter of course as those of any other physiological function;

for we should never consider a sexual act (of whatever kind) abnormal or extraordinary.

7. We should never regard a sexual act as a moral danger, for such a view is in line with ancestral taboos, and we should substitute the view that a sexual act and its consequences are beyond good and evil.

8. We must never hold abstinence from sexual acts to be a mark of superiority.

9. No sexual act may have linked with it the notion of honour, propriety, good conduct, etc. These ideas cannot apply to the bodily organs and their physiological manifestations, which are amoral or beyond good and evil.

10. The frequency and the character of sexual acts are matters for individual regulation, for personal hygiene, as are the activities of all the other bodily functions.

11. We should make it our business to ignore the sexual life of others, this being the best way for avoiding the temptation of passing judgment upon others; and we must recognise that no one can be called to account by another or by the State for his sexual activities, provided no act of violence has been done.

12. A tranquil, contented, and happy life will be secured by the free, easy, and frank performance of sexual acts. The dread which their performance or the thought of them inspires in certain persons is the outcome of an aberration arising out of artificial conventions or as the effect of repression.

In light of Guyon's concern for sexual freedom, his views on the status of women are quite
interesting. Women are, he says, sexual para-
sites; they live off of men. Furthermore, this is
an innate characteristic, fully in accord with
natural law. We cannot talk about equality between men and women, since their feelings, bodies,
and characters are so different. (This was essentially Aristotle's view.) However, he admits that
women's intellects are as good as men's, and that
they enjoy sex as much or more than men. Guyon
(1939:268) concludes: "These considerations lead
us to ask whether, in the last analysis, woman's
specific function must not always be the sexual
act--for reproduction of the species and for enjoyment. Can there be any other occupation as
appropriate to woman's nature and to woman's
genius, as are these two?"

It is important to determine whether this
kind of male chauvinism is an integral part of the
natural diverse expression model. On the one hand,
a notion of sexual freedom need not necessarily
include sexual equality any more than Plato's
Republic or Jefferson's democracy necessarily
freed the slaves. This is the problem with arguments which rely on rationalism or natural law; so
much depends on whose rationalism and natural law
one uses.

On the other hand, the umbrella of Jefferson's
democratic principles has opened wider and wider
and now, at least ideally, does cover former
slaves and women. Freedom of sexual expression
must include freedom from imposed role definitions
and ascribed status, or else our roles and status
would be prescribing how and with whom we express
our sexuality.

Guyon's person who is fully sexually expressive would seem to be self-actualized. Abraham
Maslow (1954:245-6) describes the self-actualizing
person:

Another characteristic I found of love in healthy people is that they have made no really sharp differentiation between the roles and personalities of the two sexes. That is, they did not assume that the female was passive and the male active, whether in sex or love or anything else. These people were so certain of their maleness or femaleness they did not mind taking on some of the aspects of the opposite sex role. It was especially noteworthy that they could be both passive and active lovers . . . an instance of the way in which common dichotomies are so often resolved in self-actualization, appearing to be valid dichotomies only because people are not healthy enough.

Germaine Greer (1971:142-3) quotes this passage from Maslow, then goes on to point out the problems a woman might face in attempting to be self-actualizing in a society which is still dominated by a patriarchal-authoritarian morality:

A woman who decided to become a lover without conditions might discover that her relationships broke up relatively easily because of her degree of resistance to efforts to "tame" her, and the opinion of her friends will usually be on the side of the man who was prepared to do the decent thing, who was in love with her, et cetera. Her promiscuity, resulting from her constant sexual desire, tenderness and interest in people, will not usually be differentiated from compulsive promiscuity or inability to say no, although it is fundamentally different. Her love may often be devalued by the people for whom she feels most tenderness, and her self-esteem might have much direct attack.

Greer (1973:79) also points out that sexual freedom is important for women as well as men:

". . . a one-night stand can be the most perfect and satisfying sexual encounter of all, as long as there is no element of fraud or trickery or rip-off in the way in which it develops." This is similar to the kind of sex that Erica Jong's (1973) character was looking for in the "zipless fuck."

We must conclude, then, that sexual freedom comes in degrees; but the ultimate must include freedom for both women and men. This, as Reich pointed out, can occur only when political and economic freedom exists as well. That conclusion, at least, would follow from this author's rationalism.

Albert Ellis is another expressionist who uses rationalism; but for the most part he avoids natural law. A contemporary American, Ellis has been a prolific writer in the fields of sexuality and psychotherapy. In The American Sexual Tragedy (1954), Ellis argued that Americans were terribly repressed, confused, and guilty about sex. He attempted to show how to relieve the latter in Sex Without Guilt (1958). More blows at repression were struck in 1963 with Sex and the Single Man; The Intelligent Woman's Guide to Man Hunting; and If This be Sex Heresy. . . . Then came The Case for Sexual Liberty and Homosexuality (1965); The Civilized Couple's Guide to Extramarital Adventure (1972); The Sensuous Person (1973). This is a partial list of his most popular books on sexuality. He has also published more technical works on sexuality and several works on psychotherapy.

As the book titles indicate, Ellis's views are similar to those of Guyon, although arrived at somewhat differently. He feels that most people's problems are caused by irrational thinking; his Rational-Emotive Therapy (RET) is an attempt to replace irrational with rational thinking. Among the many irrational ideas which people in our culture have are these: we must be perfect in all that we do; we must be liked and respected by everyone; there is a perfect solution to every problem; there are people who are totally good or bad; and we are responsible for what other people think about us.

It is not, says Ellis, what happens to us that causes us to feel unhappy, depressed, guilty and so on; it is the way we think about what happens to us that causes our problems, particularly when that thinking is irrational. One of the most irrational things we can think is that the sex acts which we enjoy are wrong. Another is that celibacy is good for us.

Ellis (1976:28-33) quotes a number of researchers who claim that abstinence or attempted abstinence are bad for the physical or psychic health. It reads a good deal like the previously quoted list of purported ills caused by masturbation:

> . . . numerous physical complaints, including headaches, gastric upsets, congestion of the pelvic region, and high blood pressure . . . attempts to suppress sexuality on the part of a highly sexed male may throw his visceral responses into a sort of confusion as well as create within him the most dramatic and dramatized conflict . . . prostatic congestion, or abacterial prostatitis . . . many types of unfulfilled irritative symptoms, low back pain, perineal discomfort, testicular aching, and early morning discharge . . . a great deal of discomfort in the testicles . . . chronic congestion of the prostate . . . inability to concentrate, irritability, insomnia, extreme nervousness, or more serious complications . . . neurosis, instability, irascibility, relative impotence . . . easier prey to ordinary diseases . . . in men, weak erections and premature ejaculations, impotence, prostatic and testicular disorders; in women, chlorosis, dysmenorrhea, shrinking of the breasts, and congestion of the ovaries, and in both sexes, insomnia and metabolic and nervous disorders.

61

Obviously there is a strong sex drive in humans; and the rational person would express that drive.

Ellis (1976:77-79) nicely summarizes his view on life in general and sex in particular:

> I take the still heretical viewpoint that sex, per se, rates as good and that sex without guilt rates even better. I also think that sex with guilt seems pretty bad and that guilt without sex seems much worse. Consequently, I spend a good deal of my time showing people how they can get rid of their guilt--and enjoy sex more. Some of the rules I teach in this respect include:
>
> 1. Sex, on the whole, proves unusually beneficial and remarkably harmless, unless you deliberately make it otherwise. You will find it hard to imagine any truly injurious sex activities among sensible, consenting adults.
>
> 2. Physically or emotionally harmful sex acts do exist, but they seem rare and easily avoided. Forcing another person to have sex relations with you, for example, or taking advantage of a minor who cannot very well give true consent, or behaving dishonestly, and thereby unfairly taking advantage of a partner-- these remain examples of antisocial acts, which we may judge immoral or wrong. . . .
>
> 3. Many so-called sex perversions --such as oral-genital, anal-genital, or noncompulsive homosexual relations--do not prove perverse but exist as healthy human sex behavior. We cannot label them as immoral or abnormal, except by arbitrary (usually biblically inspired) fiat. . . .
>
> 4. Some obsessive-compulsive, fetishistic, or compulsively performed

sex acts, such as obligatory homosexuality, compulsive voyeurism, or obsessive preoccupation with sex thoughts, may represent disturbances. But individuals who engage in such behavior do not behave wickedly or immorally just because of their disturbance. Instead, they behave self-defeatingly, and we'd better help rather than condemn or punish them.

5. We may call a sex act truly wrong by exactly the same rule we use for a non-sexual act--if it needlessly harms or takes unfair advantage of another human. . . .

. . . .

7. After you have done a wrong sex act, don't confuse the <u>act</u> with your<u>self</u>, damn (or devalue) your<u>self</u> for doing <u>it</u>, keep repetitively blaming yourself for it, or deliberately punish yourself for having committed the misdeed.

8. Keep in mind that your main goal in life, in the seventy-five or so years that you have to exist on this earth, can consist of enjoyment. Yes, peculiarly enough--<u>enjoyment</u>. You can pursue this enjoyment, preferably on a long-range rather than a short-range basis. You can make it largely nonsexual rather than sexual. You can enjoy involved, serious, complex things rather than the playboy aspects of life. But frankly acknowledge that you don't <u>have</u> to achieve something wonderful during your lifetime, to do great service to others, to change the course of the world. Merely try to enjoy yourself!

This rather lengthy quote also summarizes the natural diverse expression model. Instead of demanding that one <u>not</u> express one's sexuality, as

63

the control-repression models do, it comes very close to demanding that one must express one's sexuality. In terms of social control, the natural diverse model would demand that no social control be exercised over sexual acts which do not harm others. One might also expect that at least informal sanctions would be applied to those people who were not sexually active.

Although there are informal sanctions in every society, there would be few laws governing personal behavior in the kind of society implied by the natural diverse expression model. Only when one person actually harms another, or perhaps when one person somehow prevented another from becoming fully expressive, would formal sanctions be applied. This should also be true in areas other than sexuality; the individual's freedom and right to express himself or herself would be the guiding principles of society.

THE LEARNING MODELS

The control-repression models assumed that there is a strong sex drive which needs control; the expression models that there is a strong drive which must be allowed fulfillment. The Freudian control-repression and both natural expression views assume a "hydraulic" form for this drive: if the drive is not expressed in sexual ways, it will appear in other forms. For Freud the repressed drive resulted positively in civilization; for the expressionists the repressed drive resulted negatively in Fascism, neurosis, and other evils. The sex drive lacks this hydraulic nature in the traditional and sociological control-repression models. Instead it takes the form of a deviation-amplifying mechanism; like a cancer, the more it is allowed to express itself the bigger and more powerful it becomes.

Any notion of a strong sex drive is de-emphasized by the learning theorists. To some, it represents only a potential reward; to others it does not exist at all except as it is socially constructed and believed. Without the notion of a strong sex drive, then, the Freudian notion of repression has no validity. Nor does the learning theorist talk about normal or abnormal sexuality except, again, as a particular society might learn to apply those terms. Sexuality is divested of many of the qualities which have surrounded our thinking about it. Many old questions about sex are no longer relevant: "Is sex a tool of the devil?" or "What are the results of repression?" or "What form does a natural expression of sexuality take?" or "Is monogamy natural?"

Under the other models, some kinds of sexual expressions were considered virtuous, good, functional, healthy, adaptive, normal or mature; others were sinful, evil, disfunctional, unhealthy, maladaptive, abnormal or immature. Sexuality

65

which fell into the approved categories, it was assumed, needed no explanation. It was those that fell into the disapproved categories that needed study. Hoffman (1973:206) elucidates this problem:

> In asking the question "Why is a man homosexual?" we do not wish to imply by any means that this is to be regarded as a basically different kind of question from "Why is a man heterosexual?" Virtually all the literature on homosexuality is marred by the failure of its authors to take account of the fact that heterosexuality is just as much a problematic situation for the student of human behavior as is homosexuality. The only reason it does not seem to us a problem is because we take its existence for granted. However, we should know enough about science by now to realize that it is just those questions we take for granted that are the ones, when properly asked, which could open up new areas of scientific exploration. The question should really be put as follows: "Why does a person become sexually excited (i.e., in the case of a man, why does he get an erection) when confronted with a particular kind of stimulus?" If the question is asked in this way it can be seen that heterosexuality is just as much of a problem as homosexuality, in the scientific if not the social sense.

As Hoffman indicates, the sex research in the United States still accepts, for the most part, the "deviance-explanation" approach. A grant request to the government to study "Causes of Heterosexuality" or "Causes of Permanent Marriage" or "The Consequences of Marital Fidelity" or "Rates of Premarital Abstinance" would probably go unfunded. They might even make the "ridiculous grant request" file which seems to circulate within all funding agencies.

While the learning approaches can be seen as separate from other models, portions of it can be found in various control-repression and expression models. Freud, for example, certainly believed that the libido was subject to influences in the environment; repression was, in a sense, learned when expression of libido was punished by the father. Mostly, however, both the directionality of the sex urge and much of the repression seemed to exist in the interplay among the various components of the psyche. Both castration anxiety and penis envy were somehow innate and only needed to be triggered by external events. Perhaps they were part of the "race memory," a result of early species-learning rather than early individual learning. Carl Jung, at least, might have thought so.

The functionalist school of sociology assumes much learning; punishment of deviant actions by individuals would not otherwise make much sense. Reich, too, felt that repression was learned; Guyon agreed and added that all moralities were learned as well. None of these took the next step, however, and proposed that sexuality and the sex drive itself might be learned.

Mechanistic Learning Model

It was only after operant conditioning and behavioral modification principles were well established in other spheres that they began to be applied to the area of human sexuality. B. F. Skinner is the leading theoretician of operant conditioning, but has done very little work in human sexuality. Behavioral modification principles have been applied primarily in tightly controlled environments such as prisons, mental hospitals, and schools; and even then not specifically to sexuality to a great degree.

Our construction of the mechanical learning model, then, will not be primarily a review of the work of one or a few researchers. Instead we will briefly outline the principles of behavioralism (cf Schaefer, 1969), note a few applications of it to sexuality, and mention some of its implications.

All behavior, it is assumed, is learned by an organism through a system of rewards and punishments. The basic principles are these: any response which is followed by a positive reinforcer (reward) is likely to be repeated; and any response which is not followed by a positive reinforcer or is punished is not likely to be repeated. The role of punishment has been hotly debated; it has been generally agreed that punishment will reduce the probability that the behavior which immediately preceded it will be repeated, at least in the same circumstances. It cannot, however, effectively be used to teach new behavior.

A mechanistic learning model could assume either that sexual pleasure is totally learned or that it is a biological given. Following the law of parsimony, we will assume the latter for explanatory purposes. It is not the same as accepting a strong sex drive to assume that sexual stimulation can be found to be pleasurable, with orgasm being more pleasurable still. People often discover this by themselves; other times they are told. A young child may discover this pleasure while climbing a tree, riding a bicycle, or while exploring the genitals in much the same way the earlobe, elbow, or foot might be explored.

However it occurs, the pleasure has the capacity to become a positive reinforcer. A boy might discover that grasping the penis and moving his hand back and forth results in pleasure. This increases the probability that the grasping will recur. If orgasm occurs, this strong positive reinforcer will almost certainly cause the masturbatory response to be repeated.

Masturbation is not, of course, all that the boy is being rewarded for at that time in his life. In our culture, he is also being rewarded for

68

playing with trucks, playing cops and robbers, acting like Daddy and "being a big boy." He is <u>not</u> being rewarded (or is being punished) for crying, playing with dolls and doing other "sissy" things, or playing with his genitals in public.

For the girl it is a somewhat different matter. Her sensitive genitalia, being less exposed than the boy's, are less likely to be accidentally discovered. Too, the clitoris is more selective than the penis in that not just any stimulation will be pleasurable and therefore become a positive reinforcer. Direct or harsh stimulation will more likely result in a painful punishment than a pleasurable reward; and some lubrication, natural or artificial, is generally needed to more fully insure pleasure. Thus the girl is less likely to learn to masturbate, and less likely to learn to associate pleasure with the genitals per se.

In our culture, the girl is being rewarded for other things: playing with dolls and dishes (being a "Mommy"), looking pretty and making "pretty eyes," staying closer to home, covering the place where her breasts will someday be, and being "Daddy's girl." She is not being rewarded, or is being punished for, playing roughly or getting her frilly dress dirty; talking "tough" ("nice girls don't talk that way"); talking to strangers, particularly older male strangers; or sitting with her knees apart. She is less likely than the boy to be punished for crying, and is somewhat less likely to be punished for being a "Tomboy" than he is for being a "Sissy."

The behavioral system does, of course, get much more complicated. There are contingencies which operate as negative reinforcers, which are not the same things as punishments. A negative reinforcer is one which strengthens a behavior by its removal from the situation. Suppose a little girl is being scolded by her father. She begins to cry and hugs him, and he stops scolding her. The scolding is a negative reinforcer which strengthens the crying and hugging behavior by its removal from the situation. The crying becomes an escape response which gets her out of the unpleasant situation.

Sometimes the potentially adversive situation will be preceded by a cue, a signal that it is about to happen. If, when the cue appears, some behavior occurs which prevents the bad thing from happening, an avoidance response is learned. Suppose a girl has been treated roughly (adversive condition) in an attempted sexual encounter. She becomes stiff, rigid, and hostile; this stops the rough treatment (escape response). The next time a boy begins to make advances (a cue that the adversive condition is imminent) she becomes stiff, rigid, and hostile. This avoidance response prevents the rough treatment. If she always responds to passes with her avoidance response, she may never have the opportunity to learn that the pass may be followed by pleasure rather than pain. In fact the avoidance response, if carried over into coitus, may prevent the pleasure from occurring, and frigidity would result.

It was mentioned above that if a behavior is not followed by a reward, it will be less likely to be repeated. If some behavior has been rewarded but then the reward is removed, the behavior will gradually disappear; this is the process of extinction. Different schedules of reinforcement lead to different rates of extinction. If a behavior is rewarded every time it occurs (continuous reinforcement), it will extinguish very quickly. The person who is rewarded with a candy bar every time he or she puts money into a machine will stop doing so after only one or possibly two attempts without a reward. Most human behavior, however, is rewarded only once in a while for a particular response (intermittent reinforcement), which makes extinction much more difficult. The slot machine is an example of this.

A young man may make many attempts to seduce women and be rewarded only rarely; but since this is an intermittent schedule of reinforcement, his seducing behavior is very difficult to extinguish. What may keep him going until his first few successful attempts are the rewards he gets from his peer group for the attempts, his peer group punishments for failure to try, or the pleasurable sexual arousal which results even from unsuccessful attempts. This example points out another learned set of behaviors: in our culture the boys learn to make advances while the girls learn to fend them off.

As was previously mentioned, the learning models assume that there is no inherent directionality of sexual expression; in this they agree with Guyon, while not necessarily agreeing with the notion of infant sexuality. Part of the learning about sexuality includes learning how and with whom sexual pleasure is achieved. Sexual excitement and pleasure may be discovered in infancy or early childhood, but the pleasure seems to be much greater during and after puberty as various hormones make the genitals more receptive. At this time the excitement may be more easily discovered and may occur almost randomly.

Most people in our society become heterosexual because of the higher probability of being rewarded and of being in situations where they are exposed to it. Our movies, books, T. V. shows, parents and friends all teach us that we will be rewarded for heterosexuality. Other people, however, are in one way or another rewarded for having homosexual objects rather than heterosexual ones. Perhaps one of these random erections in a boy occurred while he was looking at or thinking about another boy. The thought of the boy is seemingly rewarded by the pleasure of stimulation. While masturbating, the boy thinks of the other male and is then rewarded by the pleasure of orgasm. That particular boy has learned that homosexual objects result in pleasure. Usually, through a similar process, he also learns that heterosexual objects bring pleasure. He becomes, at least temporarily, bisexual. He may or may not remain bisexual, depending on later learning.

For the person who becomes solely heterosexual or homosexual, a somewhat different process
occurs. The solely heterosexual person either had
no occasion to learn homosexuality or was punished
in some way for the homosexual behavior. For the
solely homosexual person, the reverse is true.
Perhaps, to use the case of a girl, early heterosexual experiences were unpleasant or painful,
while the homosexual ones were pleasant and rewarding. The avoidance response to heterosexuality leaves her the other, more rewarding,
option. Or she may simply never have the experience of learning that heterosexuality can lead to
pleasure and is satisfied, as are most hetero-
sexuals, with the one option that has been found
to be pleasurable.

The persistence of homosexuality in spite of
the heterosexual propaganda (both heterosexuality
and homosexuality rely to some extent on "recruit-
ment") in our culture should not be surprising.
Masturbation provides an interesting similarity;
in spite of all the preaching against it, the purported ills caused by it, the punishments applied
to it, and the guilt felt by it, it continues.
Why? Because people have been strongly rewarded
for it. They have learned that masturbation feels
good, and just like people who have learned that
alcohol or religion or reading books is rewarding,
they strongly resist extinction. A few highly rewarding personal experiences are more powerful
determinants of behavior than a good many less
personal admonitions. A few frightening speeches
about masturbation may make us avoid frightening
speeches about masturbation; but they are unlikely
to make us stop masturbating. The same thing is
true for the person who has found homosexuality to
be rewarding.

Unlike most of the others, the mechanistic
learning model leads itself to empirical testing.
Behavioral techniques work quite well with rats;
this is, in fact, primarily where they were

developed (in the Skinner box). They work less well with humans; largely because, Skinner indicates, all the variables cannot yet be controlled. Depending on the situation, behavioral modification (which is based on behavioral learning techniques) has had some success in attempts to change behavior. Shaping, a behavioral process in which a complicated behavior is learned in small bits, works well with the mentally retarded (Schaefer, 1969). Similar techniques have some success with young children (Bereiter & Engleman, 1966) and institutionalized juveniles (Glasser, 1965). Neither this nor any other technique has had much success with changing a person's orientation from a homosexual to a heterosexual one (Gagnon, 1977).

For the treatment of sexual dysfunctions (e.g, premature ejaculation in men, general sexual dysfunction in women) behaviorally oriented programs have reported tremendous success (Masters & Johnson, 1970; Kaplan, 1974). We can take the woman who was termed frigid in the above example. Her problem is that she gets very tense when she is in a situation where she is expected to perform sexually; her body is incapable of enjoying sex. What the sex therapist essentially does is to gradually teach her to associate relaxation with bodily stimulations. Relaxation and tenseness are incompatible responses; they cannot simultaneously exist to the same stimuli (Wolpe, 1969). Hence by learning relaxation she overcomes the tension and fear and can recognize the stimulation as being pleasurable. She achieves the sexual response she has learned to want.

The mechanistic learning model assumes that people are born tabula rasa, blank slates on which their behavior is written by external forces. The individual has no free will; the individual is reactive rather than interactive or creative. Emphasis is placed on discrete behaviors rather than complex behavior patterns. No importance is given to emotions or symbolic manipulation: the question is not "Are you depressed?" or "Why are you depressed?" but rather "What are you doing?" It is

for these reasons that the model is called mechanistic.

Many people fear the social control implications of this model; of course in doing so, they
are implicitly recognizing its validity. It does
not necessarily imply any particular kind of sexual
expression; it simply says that if you desire a
particular result we know the tools to achieve that
goal. In order to train people to behave in a particular kind of way, however, the environment in
which the learning takes place must be carefully
controlled. This is the only way in which it can
be assured that appropriate behaviors will be
learned.

As with the other models, then, a particular
kind of social and political structure is implied.
Skinner has constructed such a society, although an
imaginary one, in his book Walden Two. The people
are all happy; there is no violence, crime, nor
serious conflict; everyone is well-fed, well-
clothed, and well-entertained; the arts flourish;
it is the best of all worlds. But the ultimate
power rests in the hands of a very few people who
control the contingencies of reinforcement. The
behavioralists (Skinner, 1971), however, do not see
this as problematic. Since we are all controlled
by behavioral principles anyway, why not use these
principles to produce a desirable society instead
of leaving them to the same forces that have resulted in the unhappiness, wars, and tyrannies of
the past?

The Social Learning Model

The social learning model combines some of the
assumptions of the mechanistic learning model with
elements of various related branches of sociology:
social constructionism (Berger, 1963, 1966); symbolic interactionism (Blumer, 1969; Duncan, 1962);
dramaturgic sociology (Goffman, 1959, 1967);
phenomenology (Psathas, 1973); ethnomethodology
(Garfinkel, 1967); and others.

The principal proponents of this model are William Simon and John Gagnon, who worked together for a time at the Kinsey Institute and have published several books together. More recently Gagnon, a sociologist, has written on his own. His most recent work is Human Sexualities (1977), from which most of the description of this model will come. The plural title (Sexualities) was chosen to indicate that there are many forms that sexuality can take. Gagnon indicates that the plural for human would have been used also, were one available; humanness, too, comes in many forms. To understand the full implications of these plurals is to go a long way toward understanding the model.

Gagnon (1977:33) denies that there is such a thing as a strong, innate sex drive; but becoming sexual is much more complicated than mechanical learning model would indicate:

> . . . there is no sex drive or instinct. When human beings are born into a culture or society, they begin a process of acquiring the symbols and meanings of that proximate world as they learn who they are, develop a self-identity, and actively participate in assembling that self. They are purposive, intentional, and sometimes reflexive creatures. That is, they begin to choose paths of behavior. The domain of meaning and conduct called sexuality is accumulated through social learning, without the aid of a drive. People participate in shaping the environment around them, and are not merely passive objects of that environment. Cultures are part of the environment that creates and elicits sexuality. There is no innate sexual potential within the child; we create our own sexual "natures" by the meanings we give to sex.

This quote also points out the complicated relationship between the individual and society. Neither exists apart from the other. The society

75

influences the individual by providing norms, values, and roles which are often taken for granted by the individual. Individuals, on the other hand, continually negotiate these directives in inter-action with other individuals. No set of values can possibly, particularly in complex societies, cover every human exigency. The society can only furnish guidelines (although even these must be continually confirmed or rejected by individuals); their specific application must be worked out by personal interaction.

Among the guidelines provided by society is a sexual script. The individual actor in society is handed a script which defines the who, what, when, where, and why of sexuality. These scripts vary from one society to another and, indeed, within particular societies. Men and women in the same society often have different scripts; the scripts also vary by ethnicity and class. The more diverse the society the more diverse will be the sexual scripts within it, and the more difficult it is to generalize about the sexuality of that society. But even the United States, which is very diverse in many ways, has a sexual script, however broad it might be, and however many deviations from it there may be.

For illustrative purposes, the script of the traditional control-repressive model might be analyzed; it seems to be the simplest:

Who one has sex with: spouse.
What is done sexually: missionary-position coitus only.
When sex is appropriate: during childbearing years; at night.
Where sex occurs: total privacy; under the covers in the dark.
Why one has sex: procreation; sometimes one cannot control oneself.

The whys of sex in our society are nearly endless. A couple may have sex to produce chil-dren, as the traditional model suggests; but they may also have sex for enjoyment or recreation; to express or prove their love; to make up after an argument; or to celebrate an anniversary or other special occasion. An individual has whys which may or may not be the same as those stated to the partner. A young man may have sex to gain the approval of his peers; a young woman may not have sex for the same reason. A person who fears he or she might be homosexual could have sex to prove the reverse; a person who values his or her homosexual identity may have sex to prove it is true. Some women in the feminist movement are having Lesbian sex to make a political statement; some women in the antifeminist movement are having sex with their husbands to make a different political statement. Gagnon (1977:8) comments:

> The why of sex is its rhetoric. Sex is for: having children; leisure; lust; fun; passion; love; variety; intimacy; rebellion; degradation; expressing human potential/nature/instincts/needs; exploitation; relaxation; reducing tension; achievement; service. Whatever reasons people offer for doing anything else they use for sex. Some reasons are approved, some disapproved; some we share with others, some we conceal; we may tell others one thing, and tell ourselves another. We acquire the whys in the same ways we acquire our sexual techniques and sexual preferences. They fit into our scripts, they are substitutable and revisable. "I do it because I love him/her." "I was carried away by passion." "I was being used." "I was just horny at the time." "I feel emotionally closer to the people I have sex with."

The things we tell ourselves and others both shapes our sexuality and is shaped by it. This rhetoric takes the form of symbolic communication. Our ability to manipulate symbols changes as we get older. We learn new symbols; old symbols take on new meanings. Freud's concept of infant sexuality

assumed that the infant imputed the same meaning
to sex as did adults. This is fallacious, as
Gagnon (1975:63) indicates:

> In Freud sexual arousal lies in nature.
> Sexuality is preeminently a social process
> that children learn as they grow. When an
> infant plays with its penis or vagina,
> this is not masturbation as Freud would
> have us believe. The infant doesn't have
> all of the things in its head that a 15-
> year-old would have while performing the
> same physical act, or a 40-year-old man
> who has masturbated since adolescence, or
> a 40-year-old woman who is masturbating
> for the first time. These are really dif-
> ferent acts because they mean different
> things to the actors. What is critical
> about sex is not what the body does, but
> how one's psychology relates to the body.
> Getting back to Freud, you cannot repress
> what you do not know, and children, as
> children, do not know sex. It is only
> later that the grown-up child, in collabo-
> ration with his or her analyst, ascribes
> sexuality to the child's act of touching
> its genitalia. The dilemma in psycho-
> analysis is adultomorphism--attributing
> to children the characteristics of adults.

Children may, then, engage in behavior which
is defined by adults as sex play without themselves
imputing the same meaning to the act. The game of
Doctor or Nurse, in which children examine each
other's bodies, is commonly interpreted by adults
as being sex play; it might as easily be called
occupational play. The children have learned that
medical personnel have the right to examine people's
bodies; they have also learned that the doctor is
usually a man and a nurse is usually a woman, and
assume their roles accordingly.

It is not then surprising that adults, when
looking back on their own Doctor games, define them
retrospectively as sex play. Adults see children's

behavior through adult meanings; this applies not only to other's but to their own childhoods as well. When in psychoanalysis the patient learns selectively to look at his or her earlier relationships with parents through the meanings of the analyst. It would not be surprising, then, if they "discover" that they had sexual desires for their opposite sex parent. (If they do not discover it, it has been suppressed.) It is also not particularly surprising that this discovery may not help them solve the problem for which they entered analysis in the first place.

It is not uncommon that an adult homosexual will say, "I have been a homosexual all my life." That makes as little sense as saying that one has been a heterosexual or a doctor or a married person or a carpenter all of one's life. What may happen in any of these cases is that the person actually reorganizes his or her childhood from an adult perspective. What might have happened in the case of the homosexual is that he or she felt somehow different from other children, that there was no feeling of belonging to the peer group. Then after the homosexual experience, the different feeling is imputed to be homosexuality, part of the individual's self-image. For other people who have a homosexual experience, the category "homosexual" does not become an organizing self-concept; instead it may become "a normal part of growing up," or "a way to make some quick money" or "something that other person made me do."

This points out the importance of our definition of self, an importance not recognized by the mechanistic learning model. The way we perceive other people's perceptions of us, as Cooley has pointed out, is important in our construction of the self-concept. Our self-concept, in turn, influences the way we perceive the world; but it also influences the world we see. Individuals vary in the kinds of things they see as being sexual or erotic. If an artist sees a bell pepper as erotic, he might photograph that pepper in a way that leads others to see it as erotic as well. Edward Weston has done just that. His definition of the situation has influenced other people's definitions.

One of Freud's influences in the United States was to make people impute sexuality to almost everything: a mother nursing her baby; a baby sitting on her daddy's lap; two males holding hands; all these things have sexual connotations for Americans that they do not necessarily have in other cultures. When two people who are married (but not to each other) have dinner together in an expensive restaurant, other people almost invariably assume that there is a sexual significance in their actions. These two people themselves, in fact, may have difficulty maintaining their "professional" or "friendly" definition of the situation. This fact has limited close friendship almost entirely to members of the same sex in our society, particularly for married people.

Americans have also learned to look for sexual symbolism in places that might seem ludicrous to other people. "Phallic symbols" abound; the Washington monument is an example. Yet it makes no more logical sense to say that the Washington monument looks like a penis than to say that a particular penis looks like the Washington monument; or in fact to see no resemblance at all. Our movies, plays, and art have become sources of Freudian symbolism. The artists have learned to put them there and the critics have learned to see them.

There are millions of pills on the market; but to take "the pill" is to take just one kind. There are millions of things that people can do; but to do "it" is to do just one thing. There are many kinds of troubles people can have; but for a girl to "get in trouble" means only one thing. There are many kinds of solitary games in which people can engage; but to "play with oneself" is to do but one thing. Buildings, bridges, and ships can be erected, but to "have an erection" involves one particular thing. These are but a few of the examples which indicate that Americans have infused much of the world they see with sexual meanings.

This determines the kind of world they get, as Gagnon (1977:34) points out:

> . . . the kind of sexuality that members of a culture believe helps create the kind of sexuality they get. If they believe that sex is an anarchic powerful drive and teach that view to young people, then they will get at least some who will behave as if they were possessed by an anarchic and powerful drive. If they offer sex as a calming and therapeutic truth, a friendly gesture (and if they create a good learning environment, not merely holding out a set of goals without giving instructions on how to get there), then the good learners will find that sex is indeed a calming and therapeutic experience. All of social life is a part of self-fulfilling prophecy --if we teach people to believe something and tell them that it is right, then they will tend to act in that direction. However, our control of learning is never complete; people behave reflexively, and often choose not to do what we want them to.

Here Gagnon has stated the implications of the social learning model for social control: the society itself largely creates the kind of sexuality which it in turn controls. The why of rape in a society which believes in a strong sex drive is that the strong drive got out of control. When rape is defined as a deviant act, it is important that blame be established. The court trial for rape in the United States is often the competition between two different definitions of the situation: either the woman was responsible by her dress, actions, and so on for arousing the uncontrollable desire in the man; or the man was at fault for failing to control his desire. The judge or jury decides which definition best fits what actually happened. Seldom are the models of sexuality which created the strong sex drive put on trial.

The social learning model is a different kind
of model from the others in some respects; it is,
in part, a meta-model which can be used to analyze
the others. The social learning model can be used
to determine what scripts are implied by the other
models; what purposes for sexuality they propose;
and what the consequences of believing in that
model might be. But what are the consequences of
believing the social learning model itself? Apart
from describing the scripts of other models, what
script would it imply?

The social learning model assumes the position
of cultural relativity in looking at various cultures; to this extent it might lead to a functionalist approach, i.e., how does that view of sexuality integrate itself into the rest of the society
of which it is a part? The functionalist model,
however, assumes the existence of a strong sex
drive; the social learning model does not. The
social learning model is free to say, then, that if
you truly want a society without violent sex, do
not teach the doctrine that there is a sex drive
which is strong and often violent. The power of
sex in the society could be de-fused by teaching
that it is more nearly like other aspects of our
lives. Suppose, for example, we learned that having sex is like playing music: it has to be
learned, although some people are better at it than
others; even those who are not particularly good at
it can enjoy it; sometimes we play with others and
sometimes by ourselves; there are many different
kinds of music, each bringing enjoyment to some;
some do not enjoy it at all, but that is up to
them; for those who do enjoy it, their lives would
be less full without it but most would survive. It
is curious that in spite of the fact that some form
of music exists in almost every society, no one has
yet proposed that there is a "strong music drive"
in humans which must either be controlled or expressed for a good society to be possible. The
comparison breaks down, of course, when we realize
that playing music does not directly result in
babies; but then, neither do roughly 99.9 percent
of sex acts. Surely some better model could be

proposed which takes account of, but is not based solely on, that other 0.1 percent.

CONCLUSION

     If we wish to objectively examine the social control implications of the various models of sexuality, the social learning view seems the most helpful. If any of the other models are accepted, we can only analyze in terms of "right" or "wrong." The social learning view better enables us to step out of the world and to challenge taken-for-granted assumptions.

     We will first consider the concept of a sex drive, which is an important one in establishing models of sexuality. Each model has a somewhat different view of this drive. Four possible components of a sex drive, which help us clarify these differences, can be discerned (see Figure One):

    (1) Inherent directionality: does the sex drive direct itself to certain objects? The Freudian control-repression and nature-limited models would both say yes.

    (2) Sublimation mechanism: if the sex drive is not manifested directly, will it find expression in other ways? The two models in (1) above plus the natural diverse expression model would say yes.

    (3) Powerful innate drive: is there a strong, species-wide need for sexual satisfaction which would be present even in the absence of social learning? This is generally agreed by psychologists to be a minimum definition of an innate drive. The three models which agreed to (2) above plus the traditional control-repression and sociological control-repression models would agree to this point.

    (4) Innate sexual pleasure: would humans naturally recognize and label sexual

stimulation, particularly orgasm, as being pleasurable? All the above plus the mechanistic learning model would agree to this point.

The social learning model would concur with none of these points, since it sees sexuality as being learned in a particular social context. The areas of agreement are indicated in Figure One. Drive Type A agrees with all four characteristics; Type B with characteristics two, three, and four only, and so on.

Reasons for disagreement with the four characteristics will be given to round out our typology. The disagreements are, in Guttman scale fashion, also cumulative:

(1) Inherent directionality is disputed by the widely divergent forms which sexuality takes in humans.

(2) The sublimation mechanism is disputed by the observation that frequency of sexual expression is not correlated, positively or negatively, with other forms of activity in individuals.

(3) The powerful innate drive is disputed by pointing out that many people survive quite nicely without sexual expression: nuns, priests, and people in certain groups like the Shakers do so permanently; many others abstain, by choice or social circumstance, for various lengths of time with no apparent ill effects. There is no known case of lack of sexual expression being the direct cause of death in an individual.

(4) Innate sexual pleasure is disputed by the fact that many people do not find sex to be pleasurable, at least the first several times it occurs, i.e., until it is learned.

Figure One: TYPES OF SEX DRIVES

Characteristics of Drive	Drive Type				
	A	B	C	D	E
1. inherent directionality	yes	no	no	no	no
2. sublimation mechanism	yes	yes	no	no	no
3. powerful innate drive	yes	yes	yes	no	no
4. stimulation and orgasm are innately pleasurable	yes	yes	yes	yes	no

Drive Type	Representative Models
A	Freudian Control-Repression Nature-Limited Expression
B	Natural Diverse Expression
C	Traditional Control-Repression Sociological Control-Repression
D	Mechanistic Learning
E	Social Learning

87

To conclude, we will examine the consequences of various social constructions of the sex drive. It seems clear that the control-repression models assume a rather pessimistic view of "human nature" while the expressionist models have a rather optimistic view. It is not assumed that the view of sexuality causes the view of humanity, but that it reflects the more general view.

Figure Two indicates what the consequences of the various models might be. On the left side of the figure are the models as their followers might see them. Each starts with a sex drive, which can then be either expressed or repressed. In the Freudian view, expression leads to destruction of civilization while repression, through sublimation, leads to support of civilization. Repression also increases the sex drive through guilt, which pumps more energy into the system. The traditional and sociological control-repression views are essentially the same, but seem to be saying that with repression the sex drive will decrease, but if expressed it will increase. This creates a deviation amplifying loop between sexual expression and the sex drive, which only exacerbates the destructive effect of expression of civilization.

Both expression models, on the other hand, represent that repression will lead to the destruction of at least a "good" civilization, while expression will enhance it.

On the right side of the figure are the social learning model's perspectives of the other models. Each begins with civilization (or society or culture) which creates the sex drive and either the repression or expression which it finds appropriate. The Freudian civilization, then, creates both the sex drive and the repression necessary to control it. This inevitably leads to conflict. But the conflict only increases both the sex drive and repression; the only solution is neurosis and malaise.

Figure Two

RELATIONSHIP BETWEEN SEX DRIVE, CONFLICT, AND CIVILIZATION

MODEL'S SELF VIEW   SOCIAL LEARNING VIEW OF MODEL

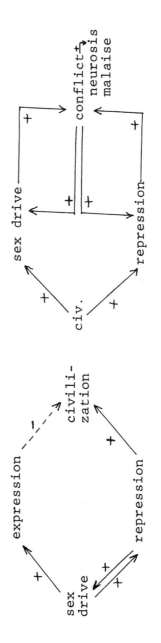

Freudian Control-Repression
Model

Figure Two (continued)

RELATIONSHIP BETWEEN SEX DRIVE, CONFLICT, AND CIVILIZATION

MODEL'S SELF VIEW   SOCIAL LEARNING VIEW OF MODEL

Traditional and Sociological Control-Repression
Models

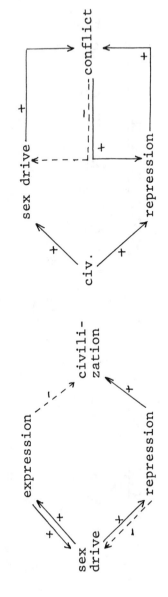

Figure Two (continued)

RELATIONSHIP BETWEEN SEX DRIVE, CONFLICT, AND CIVILIZATION

MODEL'S SELF VIEW   SOCIAL LEARNING VIEW OF MODEL

Expression
Models

The traditional and sociological models are in much the same position. There is a built-in conflict, but a partial way out is provided; the conflict actually reduces the sex drive in a deviation-counteracting loop. The conflict can never be fully resolved, however; the sex drive is continually re-created by the society. The expression models have a different outcome. A sex drive is created, but expression of that drive is also provided. The two are, therefore, in harmony.

We can now substitute "human nature" for "sex drive" in the models. The results are clear: those societies which postulate an essentially evil human nature, which needs to be controlled, will create the controls as well and have inevitable conflict; the societies which believe in a good human nature will see no need for repressive controls and will be in harmony.

REFERENCES

Ardrey, R.
1966   The Territorial Imperative. New York:
        Atheneum.
1970   The Social Contract. New York: Atheneum.

Barash, David P.
1977   Sociobiology and Behavior. New York:
        Elsevier.

Bereiter, Carl and Siegfried Engleman
1966   Teaching Disadvantaged Children in the
        Preschool. Englewood Cliffs, New Jersey:
        Prentice-Hall.

Berger, Peter
1963   Invitation to Sociology. Garden City,
        NY: Doubleday.
1966   The Social Construction of Reality.
        Garden City, NY: Doubleday.

Blumer, Herbert
1969   Symbolic Interactionism: Perspective and
        Method. Englewood Cliff, NJ: Prentice-
        Hall.

Boulding, Kenneth E.
1978   "Sociobiology or Biosociology," pp. 260-
        276 in Gregory et. al., (eds), Socio-
        biology and Human Nature. San Francisco:
        Josey-Bass.

Cole, William Graham
1959   Sex and Love in the Bible. New York:
        Association Press.

Davis, Kingsley
1971   "Sexual Behavior," pp. 313-60 in R.
        Merton & R. Nisbet (eds.), Contemporary
        Social Problems. New York: Harcourt
        Brace Javanovich.

93

Ditzion, Sidney
    1969   Marriage, Morals and Sex in America: A
              History of Ideas. New York: Octagon
              Books.

Duncan, Hugh Daziel
    1962   Communication and Social Order. New
              York: Bedminster Press.

Ellis, Albert
    1954   The American Sexual Tragedy. New York:
              Twayne Publishers.
    1963   Sex and the Single Man. New York:
              L. Stuart.
    1973   Humanistic Psychotherapy: The Rational-
              Emotive Approach. New York: Julian
              Press.
    1976   Sex and the Liberated Man. Secaucus, NJ:
              Lyle Stuart.

Freud, Sigmund
  (1905)   Three Essays on the Theory of Sexuality.
    1949   Tr. James Strachy. London: Imago.
  (1913)   Totem and Taboo. Tr. James Strachy.
    1950   London: Routledge & Paul.
  (1927)   The Future of an Illusion. Tr. W. D.
    1955   Robson-Scott. New York: Liveright.
  (1930)   Civilization and its Discontents. New
    1961   York: W. W. Norton.

Fryer, Peter
    1965   The Birth Controllers. London: Secker
              & Warburg.

Gagnon, John
    1977   Human Sexualities. Glenview, Illinois:
              Scott, Foresman.

Gagnon, John and Bruce Henderson
    1975   Human Sexuality: An Age of Ambiguity.
              Boston: Educational Associates.

Gagnon, John and William Simon
  1967   Sexual Deviance. New York: Harper &
          Row.
  1973   Sexual Conduct: The Social Sources of
          Human Sexuality. Chicago: Aldine.

Garfinkel, Harold
  1967   Studies in Ethnomethodology. Englewood
          Cliffs, NJ: Prentice-Hall.

Glasser, William
  1965   Reality Therapy: A New Approach to
          Psychiatry. New York: Harper and Row.

Goffman, Irving
  1959   The Presentation of Self in Everyday
          Life. Garden City, NY: Doubleday.
  1967   Interaction Ritual: Essays on Face-to-
          Face Behavior. Garden City, NY: Anchor.

Gouldner, Alvin
  1970   The Coming Crisis in Western Sociology.
          New York: Basic Books.

Greer, Germaine
  1971   The Female Eunich. New York: McGraw-
          Hill.
  1973   "Seduction is a Four Letter Word," in
          Playboy, January.

Gregory, Michael S., Anita Silvers, and Diane
          Sutch (ed.)
  1978   Sociobiology and Human Nature. San
          Francisco: Jossey-Bass.

Grelot, Pierre
  1964   Man and Wife in Scripture. Tr. Rosaleen
          Brennan. New York: Herder and Herder.

Guyon, Rene
  (1930) The Ethics of Sexual Acts. Tr. J. C.
  1941   and Ingeborg Flugel. Garden City, NY:
          Blue Ribbon Books.
  1939   Sexual Freedom. Tr. Eden and Cedar Paul.
          London: John Lane the Bodley Head.

Hoffman, Martin
1973   "The Roots of Homosexuality.," pp. 187-
       212 in Morrison, Eleanor S. and Vera
       Borosge (eds.), Human Sexuality: Contem-
       porary Perspectives. Palo Alto, CA:
       Mayfield.

Jensen, Arthur
1969   "How much can we boost IQ and scholastic
       achievement?" Harvard Educational
       Review 39:1-123.

Jong, Erica
1973   Fear of Flying. New York: Rinehart and
       Winston.

Kaplan, Helen Singer
1974   The New Sex Therapy: Active Treatment
       of Sexual Dysfunctions. New York:
       Brunner/Mazel.

Katchadourian, Herant A. and Donald T. Lunde
1972   Fundamentals of Human Sexuality. New
       York: Holt, Rinehart & Winston.

Kosnik, Anthony et. al.
1977   Human Sexuality: New Directions in
       Catholic Thought. New York: Paulist
       Press.

LaBarre, Weston
1954   The Human Animal. Chicago: University
       of Chicago Press.

Lorenz, Konrad
1966   On Aggression. New York: Harcourt
       Brace Javanovich.

Maslow, Abraham
1954   Motivation and Personality. New York:
       Harper and Row.

Marcuse, Herbert
1955   Eros and Civilization. Boston: Beacon.

Masters, William and Virginia Johnson
    1966   Human Sexual Response. Boston: Little,
            Brown.
    1970   Human Sexual Inadequacy. Boston:
            Little, Brown.

May, Rollo
    1969   Love and Will. New York: Norton.

Merton, R. K. and R. Nisbet
    1971   Contemporary Social Problems. New York:
            Harcourt Brace Javonovich.

Muncy, Raymond
    1973   Sex and Marriage in Utopian Communities:
            19th Century America. Bloomington:
            Indiana University Press.

Pope Paul VI
    1968   On the Regulation of Birth: Humanae
            Vitae. Washington, D. C.: United States
            Catholic Conference.

Popenoe, Cris
    1976   Books for Inner Development: The Yes!
            Guide. Washington, D. C.: Random House.

Potter, Charles Francis
    1933   Is That in the Bible? Garden City, NY:
            Garden City Publishing.

Psathas, George
    1973   Phenomenological Sociology: Issues and
            Applications. New York: Wiley.

Reich, Wilhelm
    (1930) The Sexual Revolution. Tr. Theodore P.
    1951   Wolfe. London: Vision.
    (1933) The Mass Psychology of Fascism. Tr.
    1946   Theodore P. Wolfe. New York: Orgone
            Institute Press.
    1942   The Function of the Orgasm. Tr. Theodore
            P. Wolfe. New York: World.

Schaefer, Halmuth and Patrick L. Martin
    1969   Behavior Therapy. New York: McGraw
             Hill.

Sears, Hal D.
    1977   The Sex Radicals: Free Love in High
             Victorian America. Lawrence, Kansas:
             The Regent Press of Kansas.

Simon, William and John Gagnon
    1973   "Psychosexual Development," pp. 3-17 in
             Eleanor S. Morrison and Vera Borosage
             (eds.), Human Sexuality: Contemporary
             Perspectives. Palo Alto, CA: Mayfield.

Skinner, Burrhus Frederic
    1938   The Behavior of Organisms. New York:
             Appleton-Century-Crofts.
    1948   Walden Two. New York: McMillan.
    1971   Beyond Freedom and Dignity. New York:
             Knopf.
    1974   About Behaviorism. New York: Knoph.

Tiger, L. and R. Fox
    1966   "The Zoological Perspective in Social
             Science." Man, 1:75-81.

Tiger, L. and J. Shepher
    1975   Women in the Kibbutz. New York:
             Harcourt Brace Javonovich.

Watson, David & Roland G. Tharp
    1972   Self Directed Behavior: Self Modifica-
             tion for Personal Adjustment. Monterey,
             CA: Brooks/Cole.

Weitz, Shirley
    1977   Sex Roles: Biological, Psychological,
             and Social Foundations. New York:
             Oxford University Press.

Wilson, Edward O.
    1975   Sociobiology, the New Synthesis.
             Cambridge: Harvard University Press.

Wilson, Edward O.
    1978   "What is Sociobiology?" in Gregory et.
            al. (eds.), Sociobiology and Human Nature.
            San Francisco: Josey-Bass.

Wolman, Benjamin et. al.
    1973   Dictionary of Behavioral Science. New
            York: VanNostrand Reinhold.

Wolpe, Joseph
    1969   The Practice of Behavioral Therapy. New
            York: Pergamon.

Date Due